BRIAN SCOTT

Paintings and Stories
of
Vancouver Island

I would like to dedicate this second book
of my work to my parents,
Ralph and Dorothy Scott.
I thank my Father for his never-ending curiosity
about the world, and for dragging me to the
great cathedrals, castles and art galleries in Europe
as a small boy. My Mother Dorothy has never
failed to love me, and stand behind me.
My great thanks to you both.

STORIES AND PAINTINGS

INTRODUCTION

I first moved to the Comox Valley in 1961, after several wonderful years in Europe. My father was in the Canadian Air Force, and had been stationed overseas. Free time over there was spent with my folks, four kids in tow, wandering from campgrounds to castles and cathedrals. In Comox, I had my first exposure to the spectacular fishing on Vancouver Island. After another move to North Bay, I finished secondary school and went on to attend UBC to train as an Art Teacher. I then graduated with honors from the Emily Carr College of Art and Design on Granville Island. I completed my formal education with a Masters Degree in Art Education from Western Washington University. I taught Art for twenty years at North Island College, as well as teaching for the Emily Carr College Outreach Program.

In 1979 I did 53 oil paintings on location in the Northwest Territories for Canada Tungsten Mining Corporation. This commission allowed me to purchase my first studio in Cumberland, where I lived and painted for twenty years. In 1989, I painted in a castle in Italy for a month with an Italian artist I met at North Island College. Great fun! I have also painted on the north coast of Jamaica and Maui in Hawaii. After Cumberland, I lived and painted out of Union Bay, on the east coast of Vancouver Island for several years. In 2002, I was appointed to the Board of the British Columbia Arts Council.

2004 marked my latest move to the historic farming community of Black Creek, -halfway between Courtenay/Comox and Campbell River. Here, I have opened my first Gallery. The ancient farms with tumbledown buildings, the dark fir forests, the little Mennonite kids on horseback next door are all delightful painting subjects for me!

My most recent venture is painting from Sitka, Alaska to Acapulco, Mexico; views from cruise ships of harbor scenes. A television production combining oil painting technique and the history of British Columbia is in the works. This will be a happy combination of the two great interests in my life: Art and History.

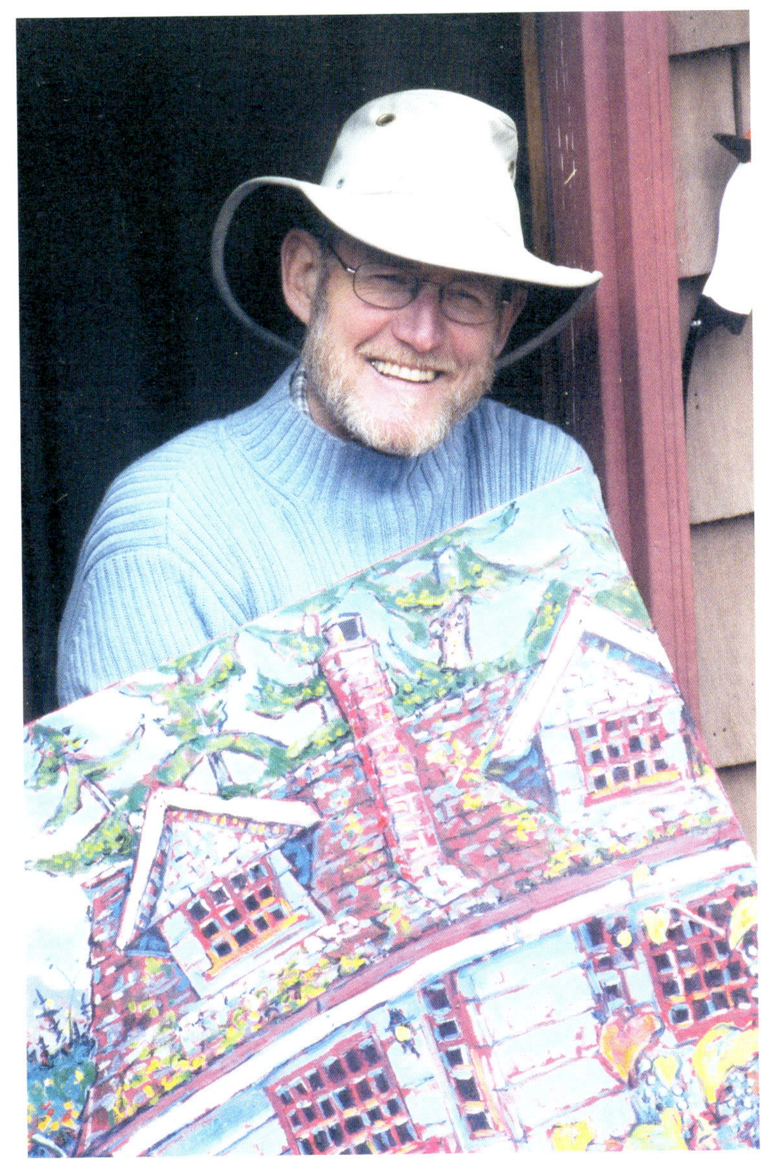

Forbidden Plateau Poppies

The Comox Glacier, the backdrop for the poppies in this painting, is probably the most dramatic landmark in the Comox Valley and possibly on Vancouver Island. Forbidden Plateau, as it is known to the local Salish Band, is significant in their history as it served as a hiding place during the recurring First Nation wars with the northern tribes.

This natural monument was created over 10,000 years ago during the last ice age. It is hard to imagine today a sheet of ice one mile thick covering the landscape! However there is plenty of evidence of the power of these glaciers. Massive rocks or glacial erratics, rounded by the slow movements of ice stand out as enormous boulders on beaches up and down the coast. The waterways were gouged out by retreating glaciers and are very deep.

Many local artists have painted this natural ice sculpture which dominates the Comox Valley skyline. In this version I was looking for the extreme colour contrast between the hot, red/orange of the oriental poppies and the cool, blue/green of the Glacier. The snow field, being almost horizontal, gives a calming effect to the composition. I also repeated the shape of the centre of the poppies in the clouds to bring the eye across and give unity to the picture.

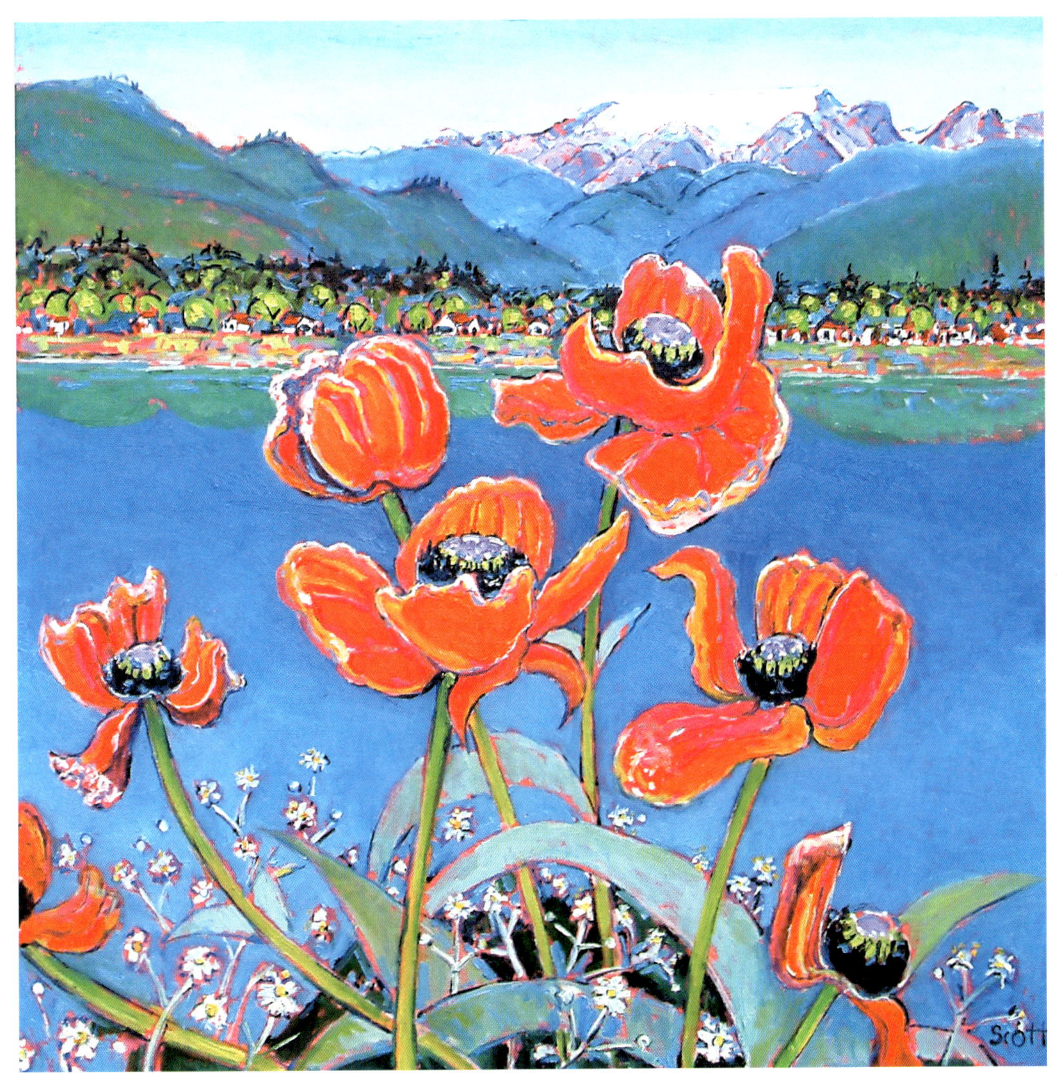

Oil on Canvas, 36 x 36 inches. "Comox Glacier Poppies"

Float Houses of B.C.

In pioneer days in B.C., being able to tow your home to the jobsite anywhere on the coast was the big advantage to owning a float house. This was common practice among loggers and fishermen. Most logging in the early days was done close to tidewater, before trucks allowed logging on higher, steeper slopes. As these stands of timber close to the 'salt chuck' were depleted, 'hand loggers' moved their float houses and families up and down the coast to the next 'logging show.' The topography of the West Coast contributed to this practice, as the mountains generally plunged straight into the ocean allowing for very few suitable building sites.

There were, however, downsides to these homes. The tide changes, up to 17 feet between high and low, could wreck havoc on a float house if the owner did not foresee this lunar certainty. Also, storms blowing out of the south-east would make living conditions very uncomfortable, or even dangerous, for float house occupants.

Float houses weren't without problems, -and these often were Toredo worms that attacked the massive log floats, turning them to wet sawdust. To stop them from eating away at the floats, the trick was to set off a stick of dynamite under the house. This would apparently shake the toredoes loose. However if not done properly, the explosion would rattle the house and all its contents. Many a wife's china cabinet was jumbled unceremoniously - often resulted in a husband sleeping on the beach!

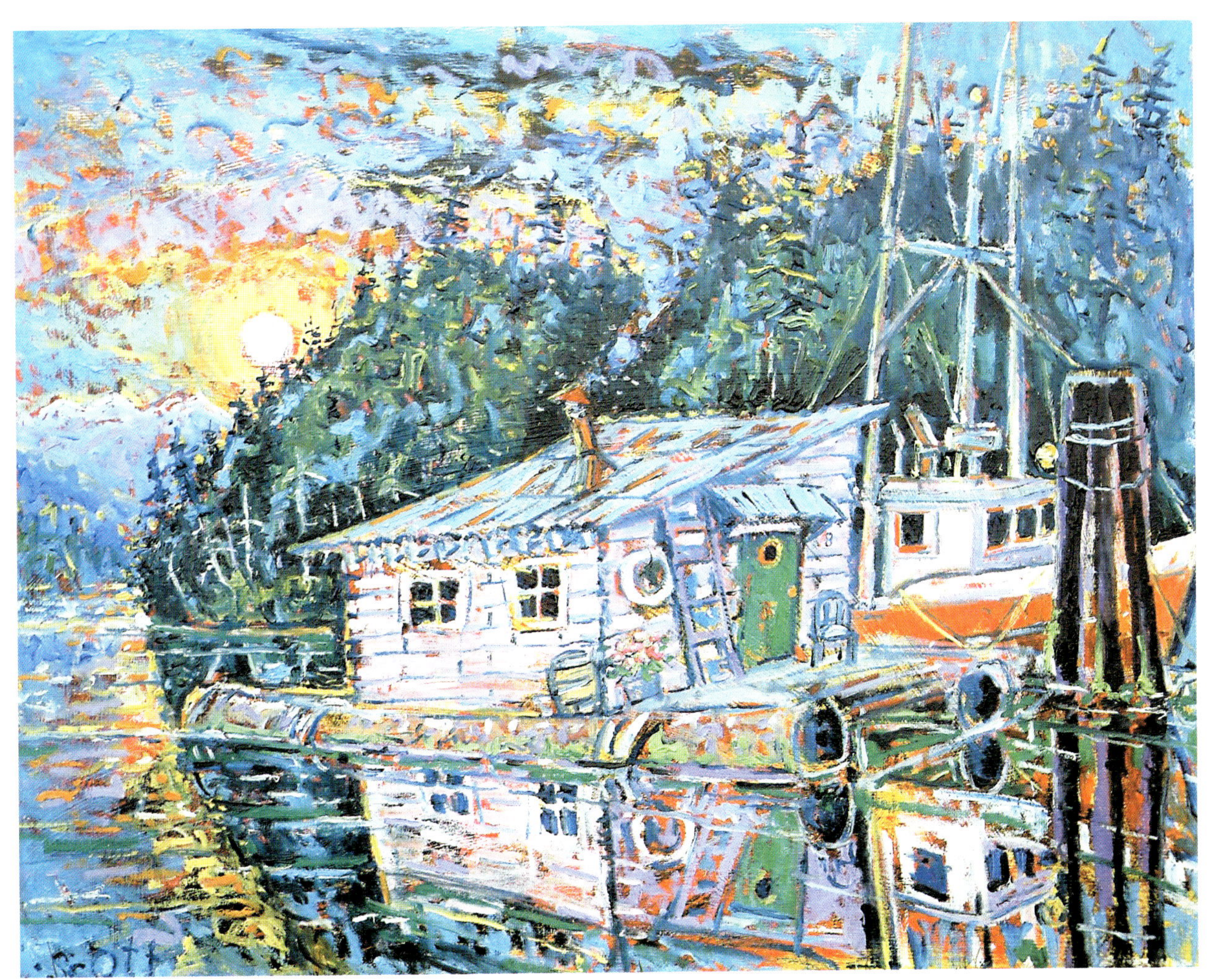

Oil on Panel, 24x30 inches. "Boat House"

"Ratz" Rattenbury, B.C. Architect

If anyone thinks B.C. history is boring, they haven't read the biography of Francis Rattenbury. This architect designed not only the Parliament Buildings in Victoria (1893), but also the Empress Hotel, Crystal Gardens as well as many Courthouses around the province. He built the first waterfront home at Oak Bay. Much of the building material for his waterfront getaway was recycled from his government building contracts. Imagine marble, mirror, stained glass and exotic woods fit for the Parliament Buildings gracing his kitchen!

Although unscrupulous by today's standards, Rattenbury was a visionary. During the Klondike Gold Rush he set up a transportation company to supply the starving miners. He even spent his honeymoon crossing the infamous Chilkoot Pass in order to promote his new company. Later he heavily backed the Grand Trunk Railway and its bid to open another Pacific terminal at Prince Rupert. This venture was a failure, and Rattenbury lost vast amounts of money speculating on land in the Skeena River region. In true Western Canadian tradition, 'Ratz' made a huge fortune, but by the start of World War I, he was nearly bankrupt.

As the saying goes, "There's no fool like an old one!" Rattenbury at age 56 divorced his wife and married a beautiful 26 year old musician named Alma Pakenham. The scandal forced the couple to leave conservative Victoria, -they fled and settled in Bournemouth on the south coast of England. The saga ends with Ratz being murdered by a young chauffeur who was having an affair with Alma, the cocaine addicted new wife. She in turn committed suicide. The young man narrowly escaped execution for the murder. This was the premier scandal of its day, making newspaper headlines around the world!

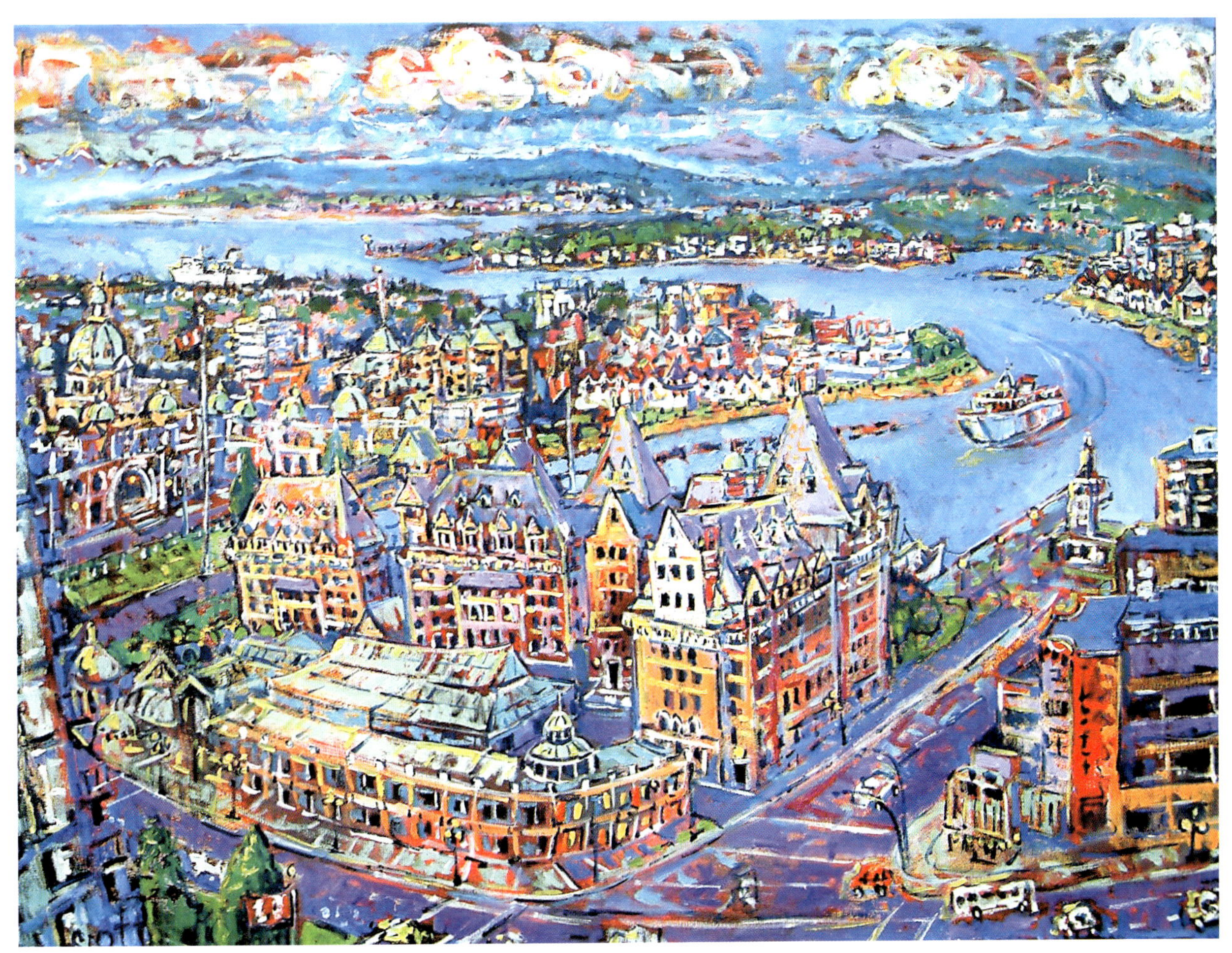

Oil on Canvas, 30 x 40 inches. "Victoria Harbour"

Sunflowers and Company Houses

The humble coalminer's cottages in Cumberland were built in stark contrast to the palatial castle built in Victoria by the coal mine owner, -Robert Dunsmuir. Today, fabulously wealthy people may choose to live in quietly understated homes. But in 19th Century Victoria, the more money you had, the bigger you built your home! Dunsmuir's mansion stood out 'like a sore thumb' on a hilltop. In Cumberland, the little homes were largely identical, hugging the hillsides down rambling little roads, with very little to distinguish one from another. Individuality was usually only evident in the variety of little gardens or window boxes loving tended by miner's wives. Only a few struggling plants could made all the difference in a row house, -made the tiny shacks feel like home.

In this painting I use the sunflowers as the symbol for the families: the wizened old grandmother stooped and grey, the strong mothers trying to keep the family together, -the boisterous teenagers reaching for the sun. When the Village celebrated its Centennial, they issued a medal to anyone who lived Cumberland for more than 80 years. The recipients were mostly the Grandmothers who had kept the town intact. They strutted their medals proudly!

There are romantic images of life in the previous century in B.C. but the more you read, you discover the brutal reality. Over the years, 650 coal miners lost their lives in the mining disasters on Vancouver Island. In those days there was no social safety net for the families left behind so a sense of community solidarity was crucial. The little rows of identical houses in Cumberland held great comfort in sudden sorrow.

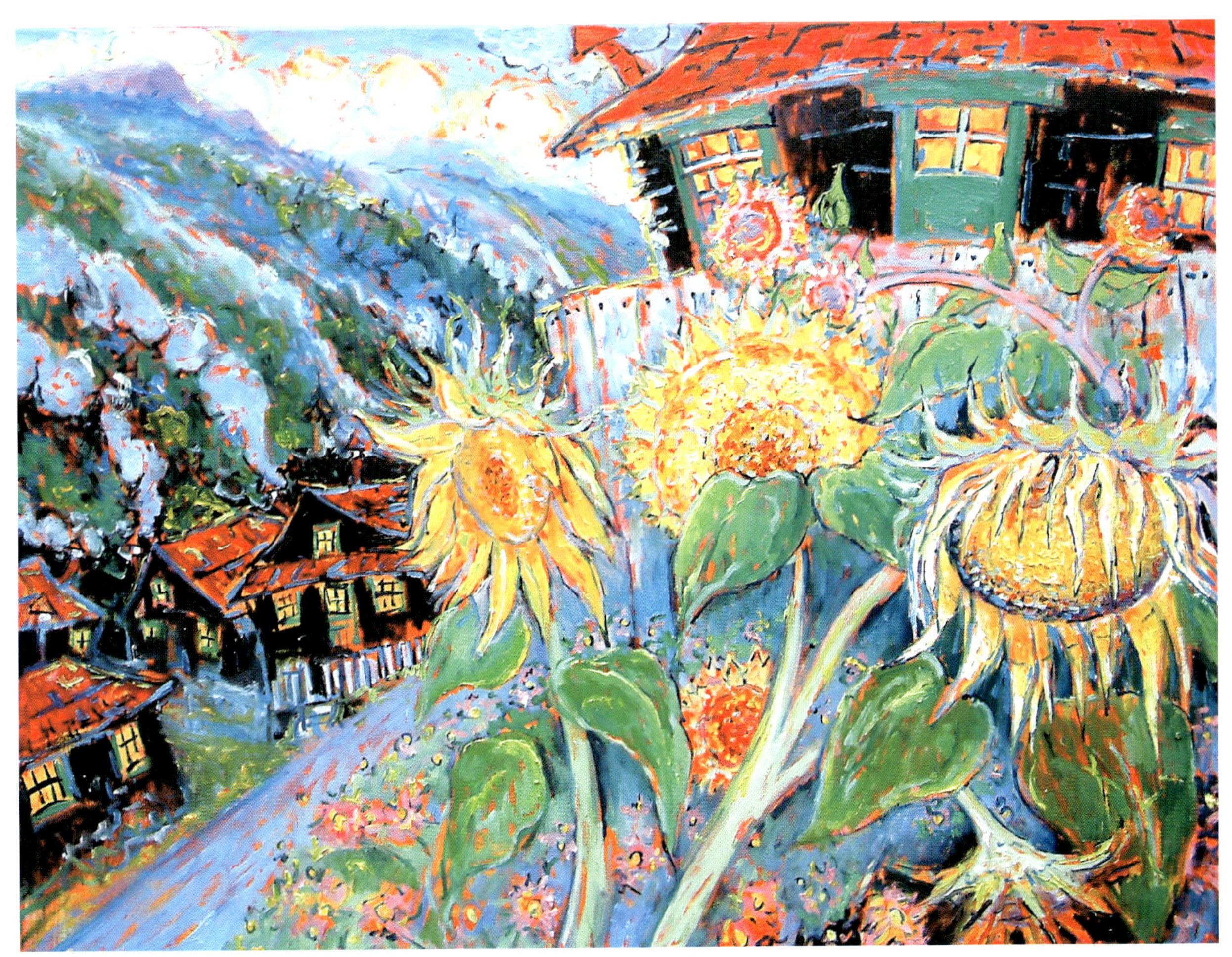

Oil on Canvas, 30 x 40 inches. "Sunflowers Coal Town"

Esquimalt and Nanaimo Railway

The Government of British Columbia in the 19th Century was desperate for a railway to connect the remote communities on Vancouver Island. The building of the Cariboo Trail to the Gold Fields had left the Province almost broke so they turned to the wealth of Robert Dunsmuir for private help. Dunsmuir was a shrewd Scot and he drove a hard bargain. In exchange for building the rail line from Victoria to Nanaimo and on to Courtenay, he received massive land, timber and mineral grants on the east coast of Vancouver Island. The railway was built in record time and was a marvel of 19th Century engineering, spanning massive gorges and rivers along its route.

When the railroad was complete, Sir John A. MacDonald, Prime Minister of Canada made the trip west to open the new Island rail link. A grand reception was planned however there was to be no booze served. The railroader's wives had been firm on this issue. However Dunsmuir, as usual, was ahead of the game and took Sir John A and his entourage on a tour of the underground coal mines. The wives in their Victorian finery were of course, excluded and the men found plenty of Scotch whiskey underground much to the wives horror.

My favorite time of year is depicted in this painting of the "E and N Railway", when the maples turning in their fall colors arch over the tracks creating a tunnel effect. When looking from the train, you view a kaleidescope of colours as the maples flash by the windows and salmon rivers cut a swath through the forests.

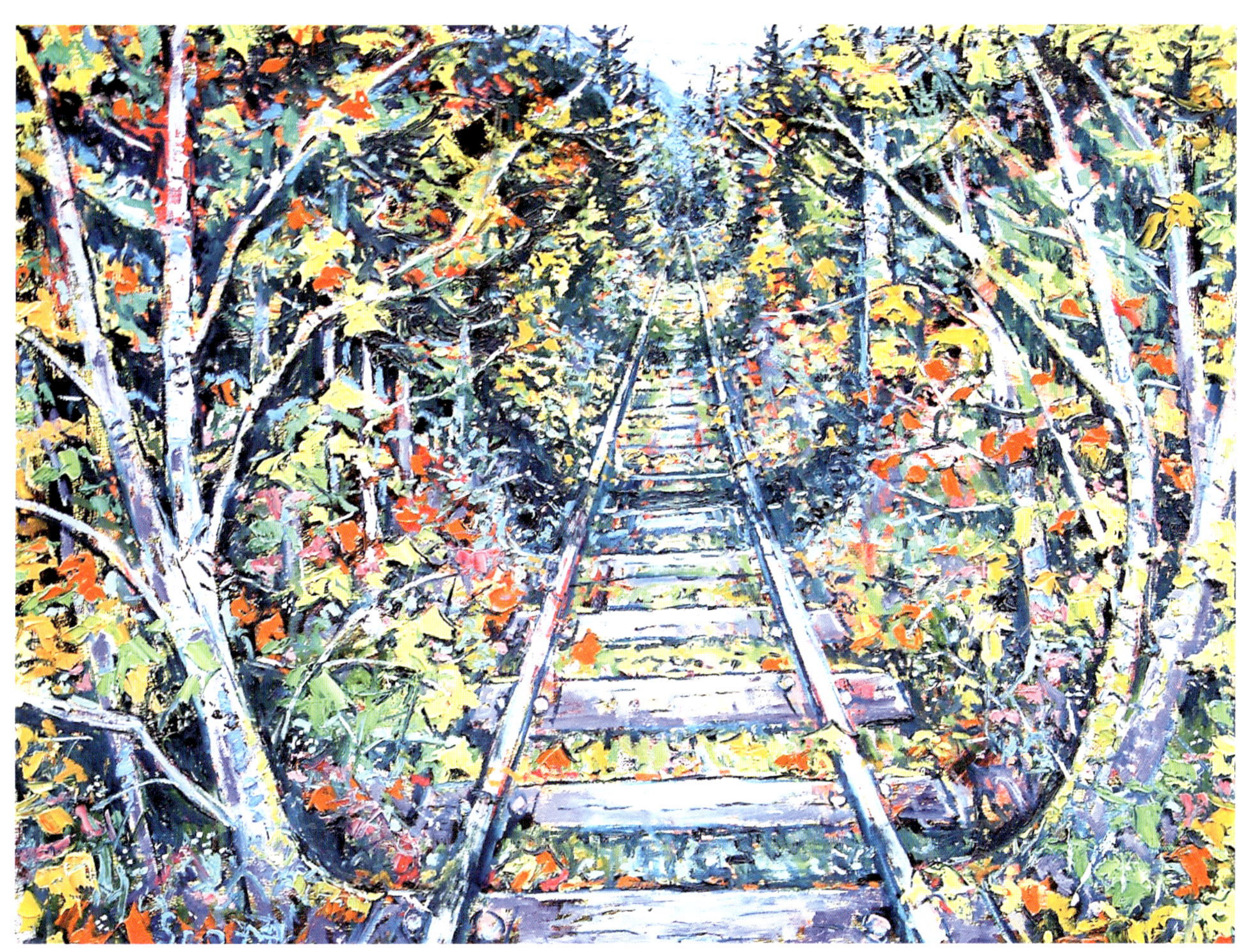

Oil on Panel, 30 x 40 inches. "E & N Railway"

Craigdarroch Castle

Robert Dunsmuir was one of the richest man in British Columbia history and a Premier of the province in the 19th Century. He started out as an indentured or contracted coal miner with the Hudson Bay Company at Fort Rupert on the north end of Vancouver Island in the 1850's. Eventually, together with his wife and family, he moved to Nanaimo and developed the high grade coal deposits that fueled the steam ships and railways of the day. Coal was king and Dunsmuir became the 'Laird' of Vancouver Island.

After many hardships in Nanaimo, Dunsmuir settled in Victoria. To reward Mary, his wife and unfailing supporter who had endured incredible hardships during their marriage, he built Craigdarroch Castle in Victoria. Dunsmuir was a controversial figure both in business and politics but one cannot fault his pioneering spirit and capacity for hard work and self denial to build a family fortune.

However, he died before the Castle was complete, and his wife lived on there without him. The couple had produced many daughters. These girls married British Naval Officers who upon marriage promptly retired from the military to live off the rapidly dwindling Dunsmuir fortune. Craigdarroch Castle was eventually also used as a Hospital, School Board Offices and has since been turned into a Museum.

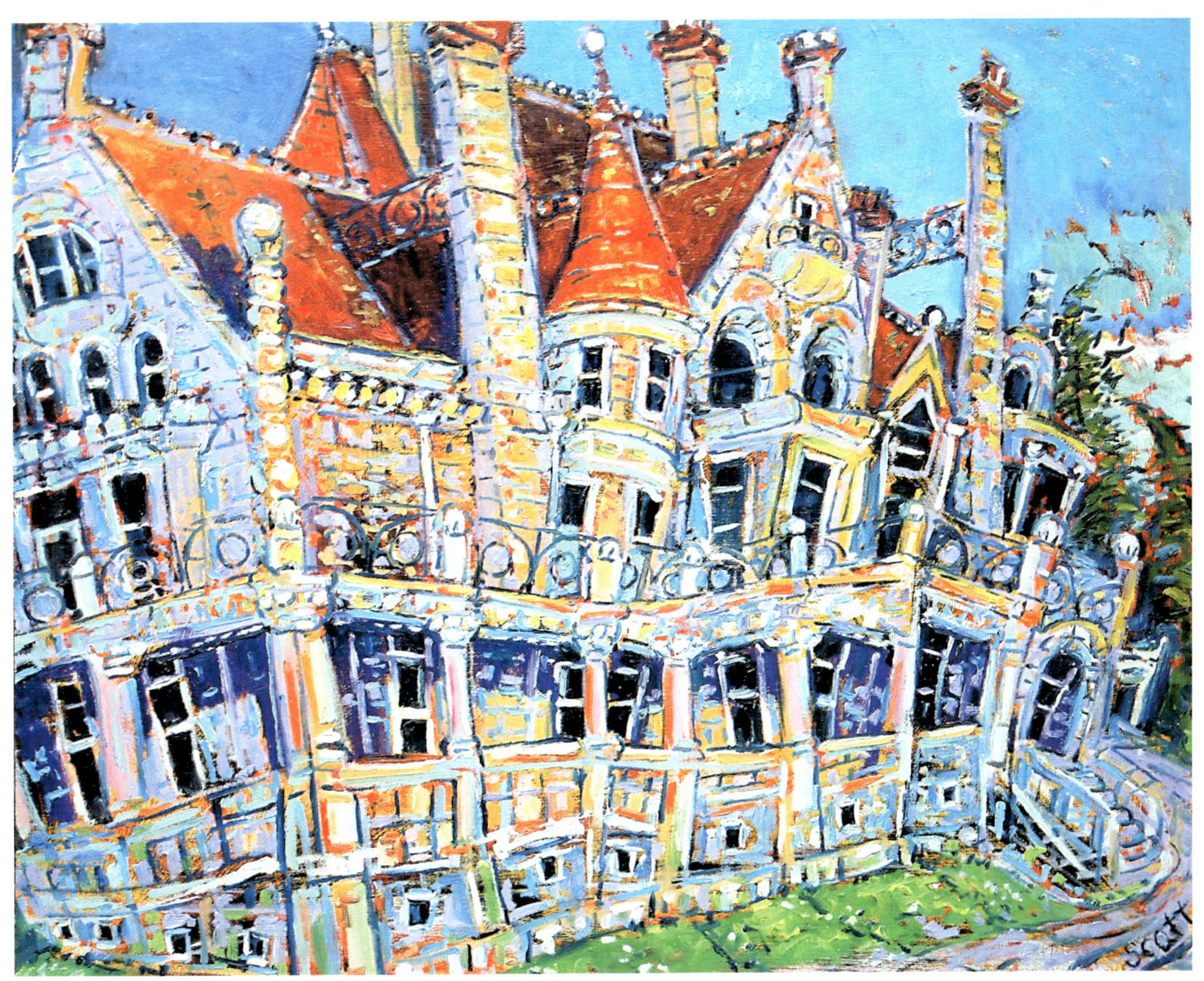

Oil on Panel, 24 x 30 inches. "Craigdarroch C."

Days Gone By '49 Ford

This painting is of my studio in Cumberland B.C. where I lived and painted for 20 years. In 1979 I did a major commission for Canada Tungsten Mining of their operations in the Northwest Territories. The paintings hang in their main office in Vancouver. The money from this project bought my Cumberland studio.

During my 20 years in Cumberland I did over 1000 paintings which I sold world wide. The biggest sale was Husky Injection Moldings Company for their Asia Pacific office in Hong Kong. Interesting that a Canadian company in Hong Kong would hang paintings of Cumberland in their office. I can only guess that the farther you get from home, the more nostalgic you become for your own country. Cumberland could be any small town in Canada so images of the town had a big emotional impact on Canadians working overseas. Jeff MacDonald, Manager of the Hong Kong office visited Cumberland and loved the quaint Victorian village.

I had often admired a derelict 1949 Ford in my neighbors yard. One day I noticed it was for sale! Apparently the old truck clashed with his wife's flower garden plan and since I didn't have a wife or a garden I asked the guy to tow it to my backyard. It was the best model I ever had, -it never talked back and didn't move for 5 years! I painted the old wreck in different seasons, but my favorite time was the Fall when the big leafed Vancouver Island maples turned yellow and gold and lay on the rust of the truck.

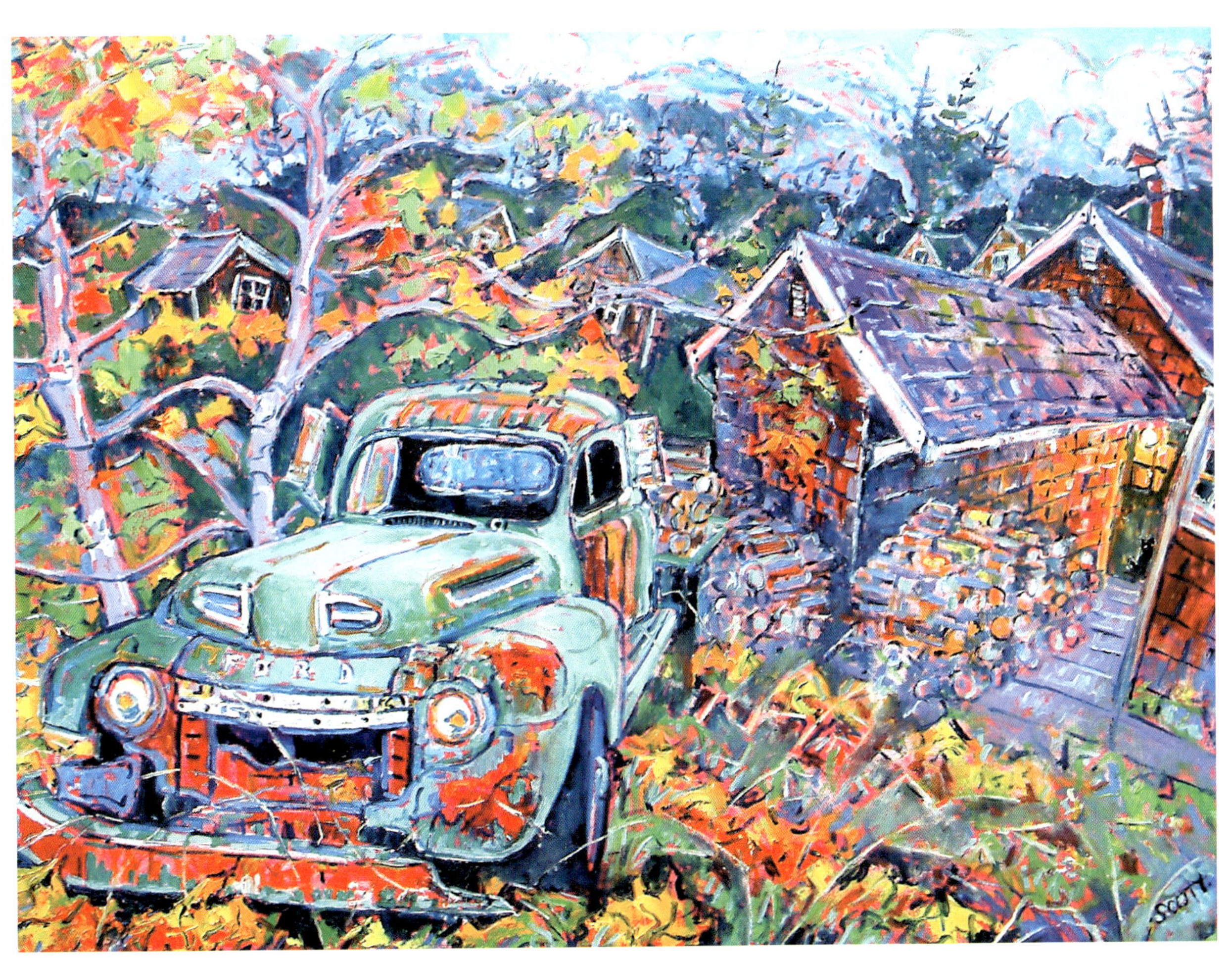

Oil on Canvas, 30 x 40 inches. "'49 Ford"

Massey Harris Tractor and the Hornby Bakery

The old tractor outside the Bakery on Hornby Island is a major remnant of Canadian History. The manufacturer, Massey Harris, was Canada's flagship international company from the 1920's into the 50's. A home-grown hero, that tractor was built tough enough to survive Canadian winters and could make it anywhere on the planet, even Siberia.

This made both the Massey and Harris families very wealthy. They were among the leading entrepreneurs of their day and their offspring benefited. Lauren Harris helped finance the Group of Seven movement which revolutionized art in Canada. Canadians became aware of the beauty of their own country through the Group of Seven's eyes. Until this time Canadian paintings had looked like modified landscapes from Europe. The Group worked initially from railway cars on location in Algonquin Park and then branched out across Canada and up into the Arctic.

Vincent Massey became Governor General of Canada and was a patron to many Canadian artists, notably David Milne. Massey at one time bought the entire body of Milne's work, helping the artist immeasurably. His brother Raymond Massey was a well known film and television actor in Hollywood.

Generations of Hornby Island children have played on this tractor not knowing its amazing pedigree! The pizza is foremost on the kid's minds as the mothers scramble in the inevitable line-up. Their rough and tumble play has left the old Massy-Harris tractor picked bare, spartan and reflective, making it an ideal subject for a painting on a summers day.

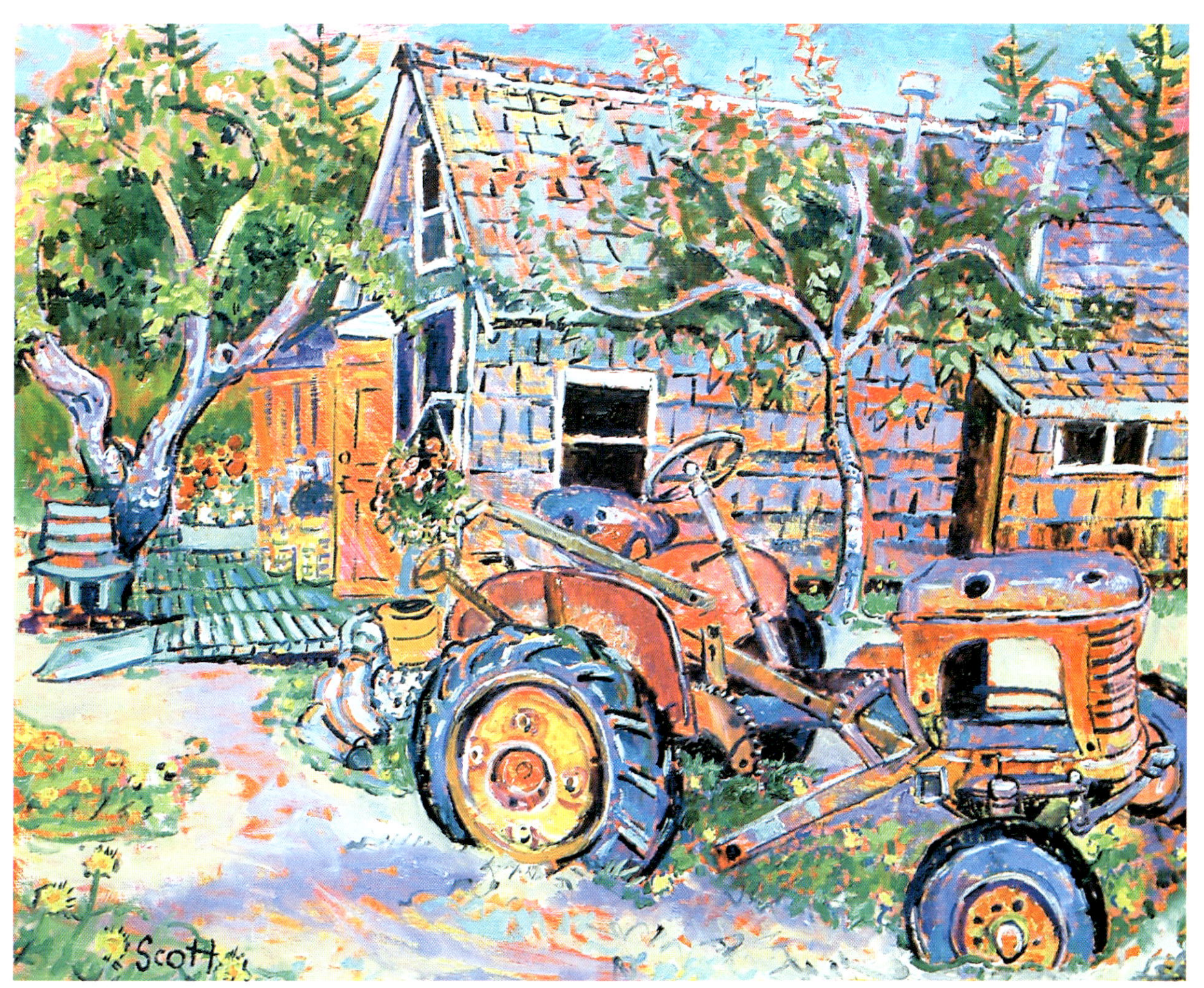

Oil on Panel, 24 x 30 inches. "Massey Harris"

Dorothy and Her Purple House

Spring in Cumberland in the Comox Valley is a riot of yellow dandelions! They're a delight for the artist, but a miserable scourge to the gardeners. Rain and sunshine pop out spring weeds in profusion!

Purple and yellow, complimentary colors, attract and repel each other at the same time. Similarly Dorothy, Cumberland's famous "Purple Lady" and her husband back in the 1950's, shared both an attraction and repulsion! When her husband was away from Cumberland working in the bush, Dorothy painted the whole house a violent purple

The village was in shock. No one had ever painted their house such wild colors in a conservative mining town! When her husband returned there was a huge ruckus and he left town. She told everyone that would listen that as she couldn't get a divorce in the 1950's she had to resort to painting the house purple to get him to leave town.

Mrs. Mauve, as Dorothy was also known, was a town character, but she commanded respect as someone who had found a novel solution to her domestic problem.

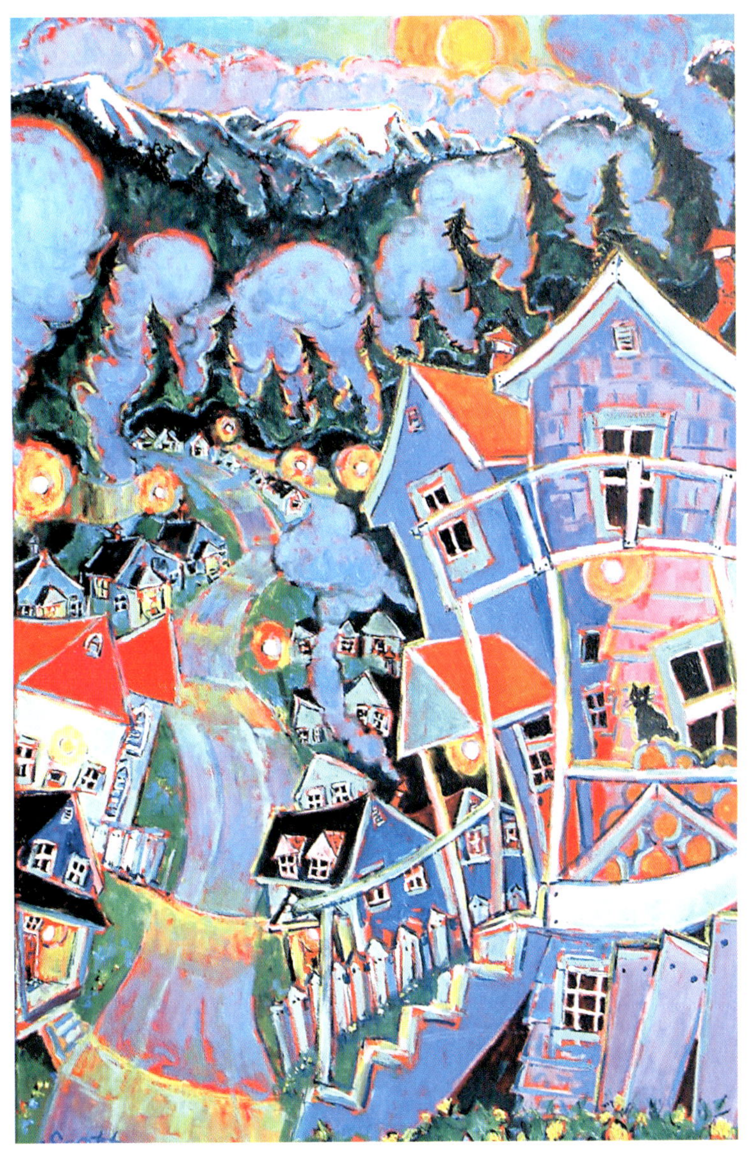

Oil on Canvas, 24 x 36 inches. "Purple House Daffodils"

Doris, Cat Lady of Cumberland

Doris Goldscheider and her husband Herbert were my first patrons. They not only purchased my early paintings but Doris fed me wonderful meals of goulash with German beer to wash them down. Born in Germany, Doris ended up in Cumberland on Vancouver Island via Chicago and Los Angeles where she had been an Art Supervisor.

In her home Doris had a massive shelf of art books. One book in particular inspired me to paint Cumberland and its vanishing history. Doris had a copy of Leo Politi's book of watercolours and stories of Bunker Hill, were there had been wonderful old Victorian houses in what is today downtown Los Angeles, now all concrete and glass. His work records the lost history of that city in the 19th century, the original Melrose Place.

On cold gloomy winter nights as a starving artist in my miners shack/studio, I dreamed of being reincarnated as one of Doris's pampered cats. They were spoiled rotten, got very fat and were lazy. Doris fed them well, -carefully chopped up bacon for them every morning! Being a good vegetarian or 'granola head', the bacon that I craved was definitely verboten! Those lucky felines, full and mischievous were free to roam in her wild and tangled garden with its bugs, birds and cherry trees.

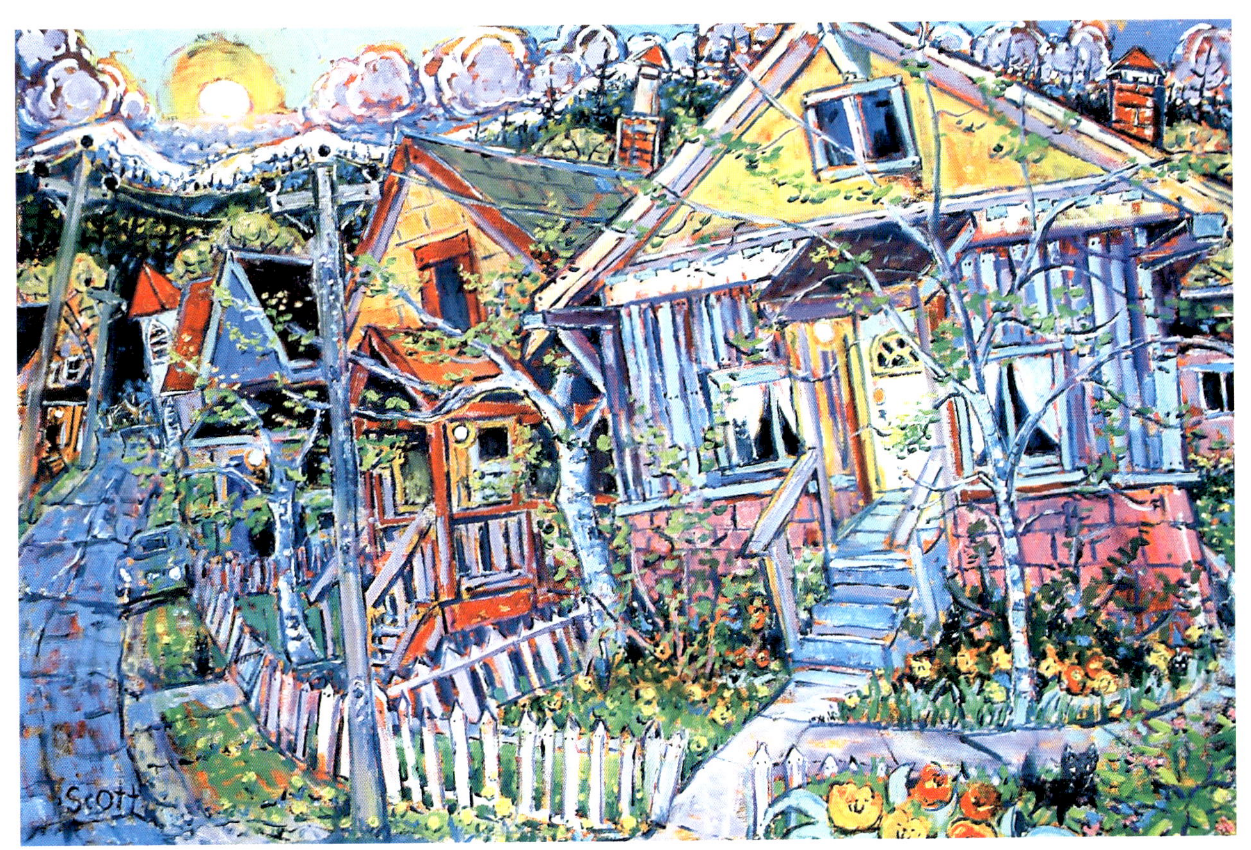

Oil on Canvas, 24 x 36 inches. "Cat House Cumberland"

Hilary Brown and Island Garden Tours

Many communities on Vancouver Island have garden tours. These take place mainly during the months of May and June, when West Coast gardens are at their peak. Rhododendrons are particularly spectacular in their many varieties and colors at this time of the year.

Gardeners are also Artists when you think of the emotion they generate by the variety of colors and forms. No two gardens are alike, although like artists, gardeners inspire each other and love to talk with great passion about their projects.

Each garden is unique and the personality of the gardener comes through in the work. The overall design is important in making a coherent statement in a formal garden. Similarly, in visual art you have the Formal Artist as well as the more Expressionist, -in West Coast gardening lingo, the "English Garden". In my experience, formal gardens tend to be more rigid, with open controlled space and hard edges, whereas the expressionist garden is more closed-in, with a myriad of paths and arbors and a profusion of colors and textures.

Most successful gardens take years to develop and one of my favorites is Hilary Brown's garden on Hornby Island at Heron Rocks. Hilary's husband, Harrison, was working as a journalist in Berlin during the 1930's and was also a fervent socialist. He was not popular in right wing Nazi Germany. Sensing a coming world war, the couple toured North America warning people about the impending world catastrophe. Largely ignored by listeners, they retreated to Hornby Island. When you think of where to escape a world war, the Gulf Islands would be an ideal sanctuary.

Their garden remains a joy, a Hornby Island treasure.

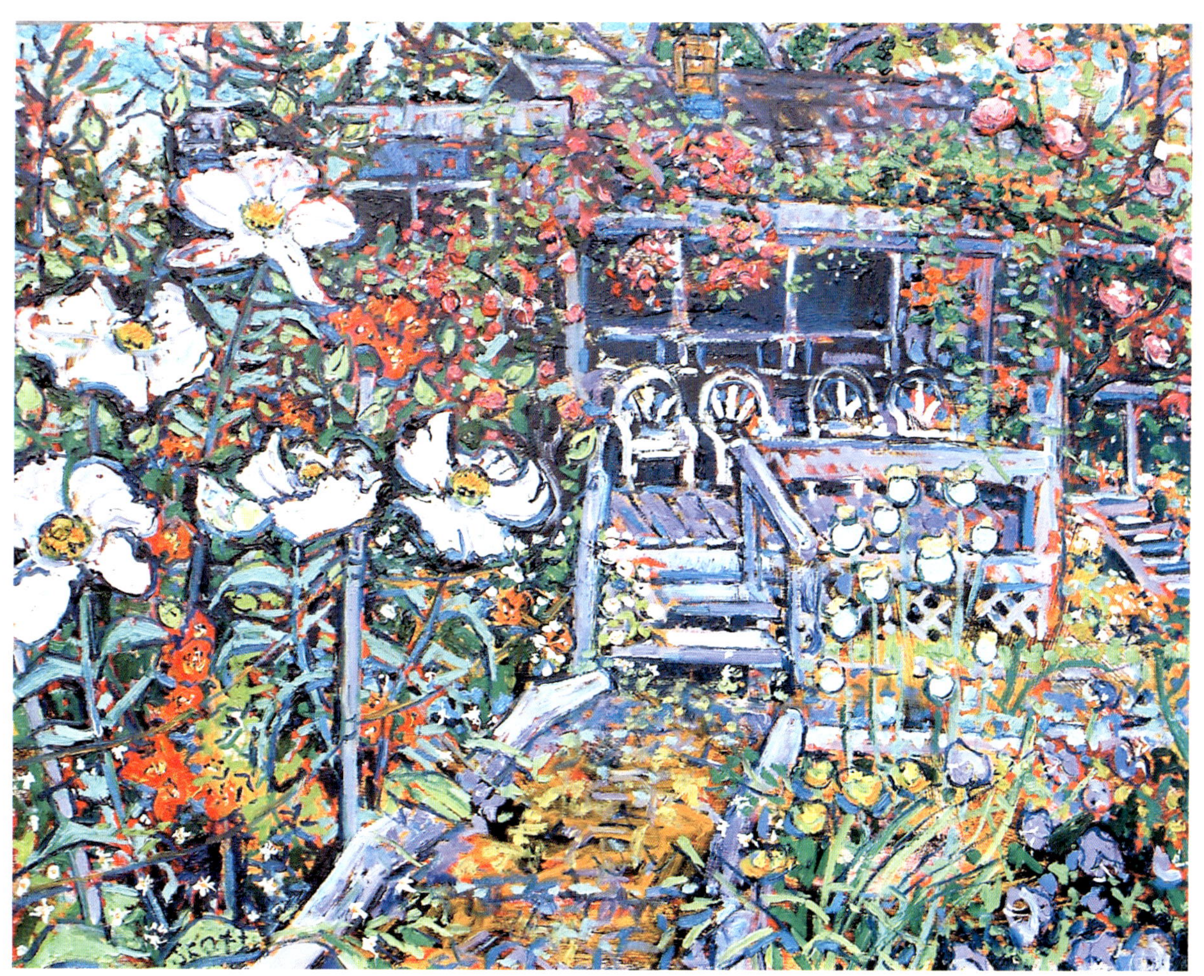

Oil on Panel, 24 x 30 inches. "Hilary Brown House"

Sybil Andrews Cottage, Willow Point

The astounding increase in value of Sybil Andrews Lino-block prints and paintings has been a windfall for many art collectors in B.C. Sybil was typical of creative personalities who fled to Vancouver Island for its solitude and beauty. Sybil came from a privileged family in Norfolk, England and married Walter Morgan, -a handsome machinist who was however below her 'station' in class conscious Great Britain. After the war, they chose instead to move away to the 'colonies' and create a new fresh life for themselves. They ended up in Campbell River, settling just south of the town in Willow Point.

Amazingly Sybil survived as an artist and teacher and is now internationally known for her lino prints. Her work and tools are featured in the prestigious Glenbow Museum in Calgary, Alberta, and in the Tate Gallery in London. She has left a legacy of dedicated students that carry on her ideas and passion for art. Her book "The Artist's Kitchen" reflects her philosophy as an artist and her unfettered approach to life.

The controversy of Sybil Andrews lives on with her waterfront studio/cottage often being threatened with demolition. Modern civil servants abhor old buildings that require maintenance and don't pay taxes. Fortunately there are sufficient numbers of locals who recognize the importance of cultural heritage and fight to keep Sybil's cottage from the wrecking ball. Her simple cottage reflects an earlier simpler lifestyle quickly disappearing on Vancouver Island. Fame and fortune were at the bottom of Sybil's list of goals. Wisdom, simplicity and an freedom to be passionate about one's art was paramount.

Sybil's cottage reminds me of earlier times where consumerism was minimal, -mass media and technology were virtually nonexistent. She lived a happy and contented life with Walter in her cottage by the sea "forever a piece of England".

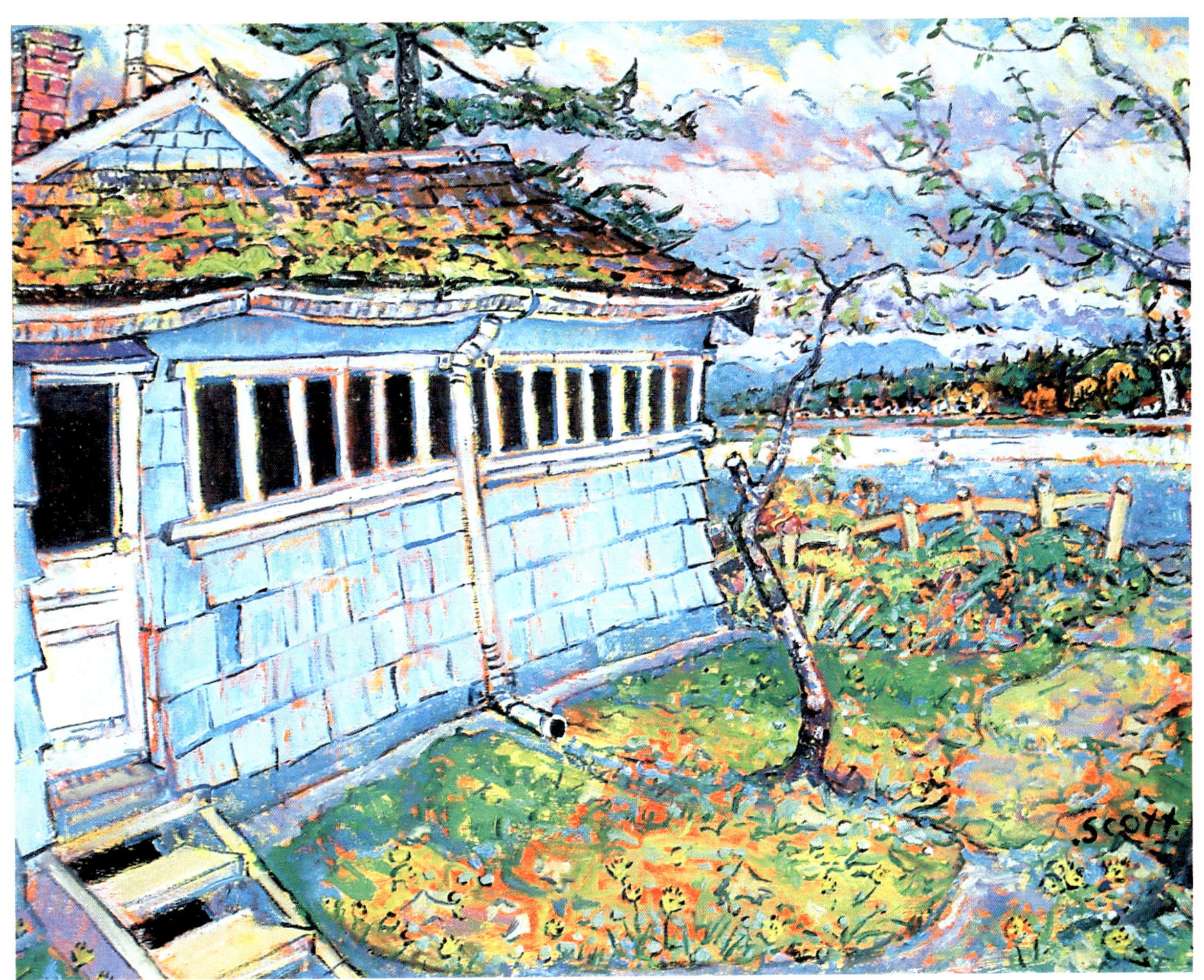

Oil on Panel, 24 x 30 inches. "Lighthouse from Sybil Andrews"

Manure Spreader

A friend of mine, a Vancouver criminal lawyer, chose a version of the "Manure Spreader" on his office wall. His clients include marijuana growers who cultivate on the wrong side of the law. Marijuana is the biggest agricultural cash crop in British Columbia, so inevitably, my lawyer friend is kept busy trying to defend these guys.

The painting of the "Manure Spreader" saves this particular law firm a lot of wasted time. If the conversation in the office strays too far from legal reality, the client is made aware of the "farm machinery" on the wall and its implications. Apparently, it helps to keep the discussion focused.

Manure spreaders like this one, and their modern counterparts, are very important on Vancouver Island since many of the farms have large dairy herds. Recycling wastes from cattle is a big part of the farming operation. When that "farm smell" is in the air you know this essential piece of farm machinery is at work!

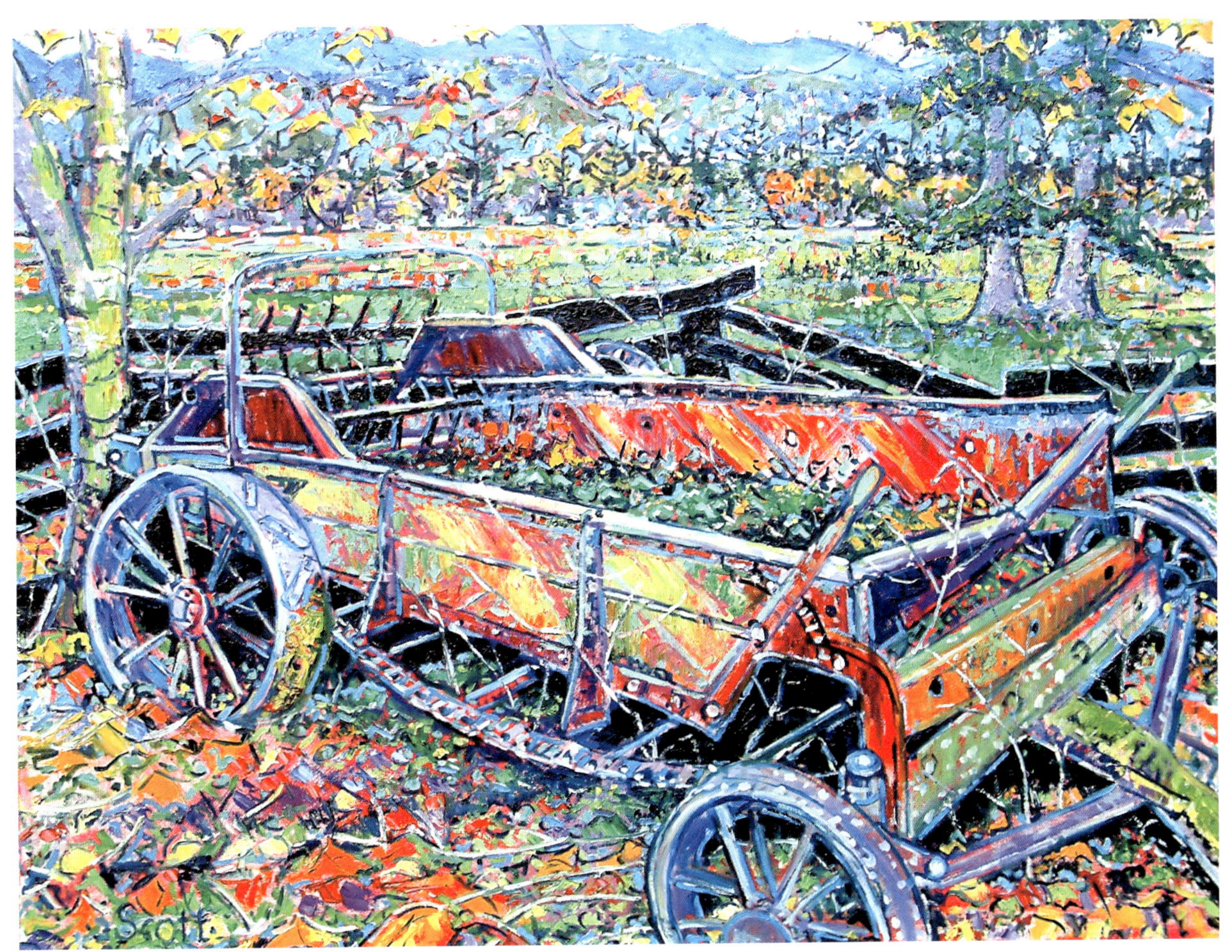

Oil on Canvas, 36 x 48 inches. "Manure Spreader Spring"

Chimney Smoke, Vancouver Island

Most of Vancouver Island is densely forested. Many people in the hinterlands have wood burning stoves to heat their homes in winter. A crackling Red Cedar fire adds cheerful music, light and heat on a rainy West Coast evening.

From my perspective, wood smoke coming from a chimney indicates a family at home. The smoke breaks up the landscape as it hangs in the forest and mixes with low lying clouds and mist. This adds contrast, both in color and form to paintings. Smoke can also be symbolic of spirits or ghosts of past inhabitants. Wood smoke is fluid, adding rhythm to the painting, an essential in any dynamic landscape work.

In pioneer days, marriageable women were scarce on Vancouver Island. Women could pick and choose from any number of available men. One strong indicator was the size of a bachelor's woodpile. Since wood was the only source of heat, a five year supply was the idea. A large wood pile guaranteed a cozy winter, and indicated the prospective husband was a hard worker, and certainly not idle!

Even today, some of the old timers on the Islands keep a five year supply of firewood at the ready. At four cords per winter, that's 20 cord of firewood, enough to cover a quarter acre of land. Forget about a lawn mower, -there's no need. There's no lawn!

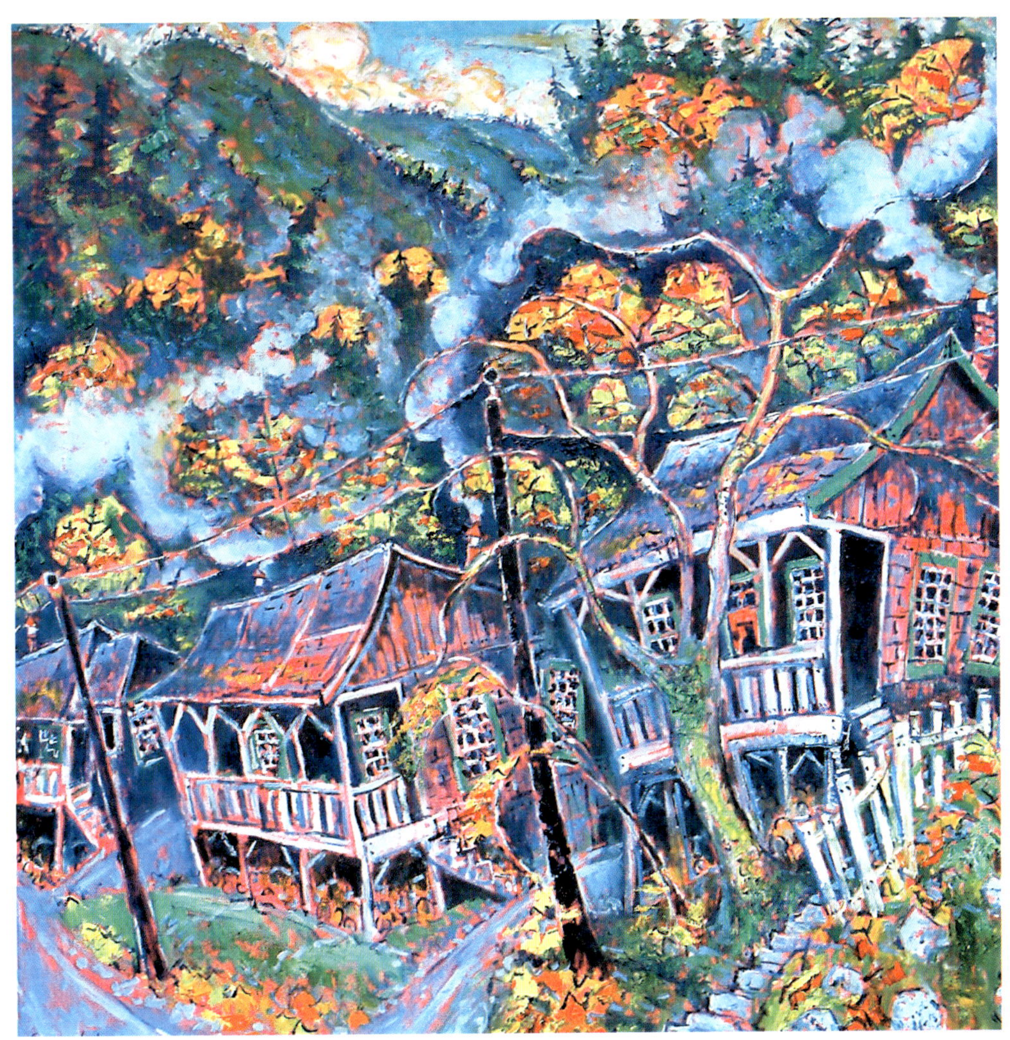

Oil on Canvas, 36 x 36 inches.

Vancouver Island Rivers

My first encounter with a Vancouver Island river was the Puntledge River. In 1961, at 12 years of age, I spent the summer rafting with inner tubes, swimming and fishing on this spectacular river. Fed by Comox Lake, which in turn is fed by the Glacier, the Puntledge is crystal clear with many pools, rapids and waterfalls. It is a virtual West Coast "Garden of Eden" for kids and artists.

The seasonal changes of the Island rivers are quite dramatic. The major salmon run begins in July with each species entering sequentially so they are not all in the river at the same time. In summer the river is slow and meandering whereas the winter runoff is violent and dangerous, claiming lives of the unwary. The fall is the most dramatic when salmon migrate up the river in schools of thousands of fish. The Northern Coho are the last actual salmon to spawn, followed by Winter Steelhead, which are trout who live primarily in the ocean but, like salmon, spawn in the rivers. Each species takes its own turn in these magnificent waterways.

Most of the names come from the Indian Bands that lived along the river banks such as the Nimpkish, Cowichan, Puntlatch, Qualicum, and Nanaimo. Other names like the Trent and Englishman originated from homesick surveyors and pioneers who left their place of origin's name on the local rivers.

Island rivers are part of the magnificent complexity and beauty in this area.

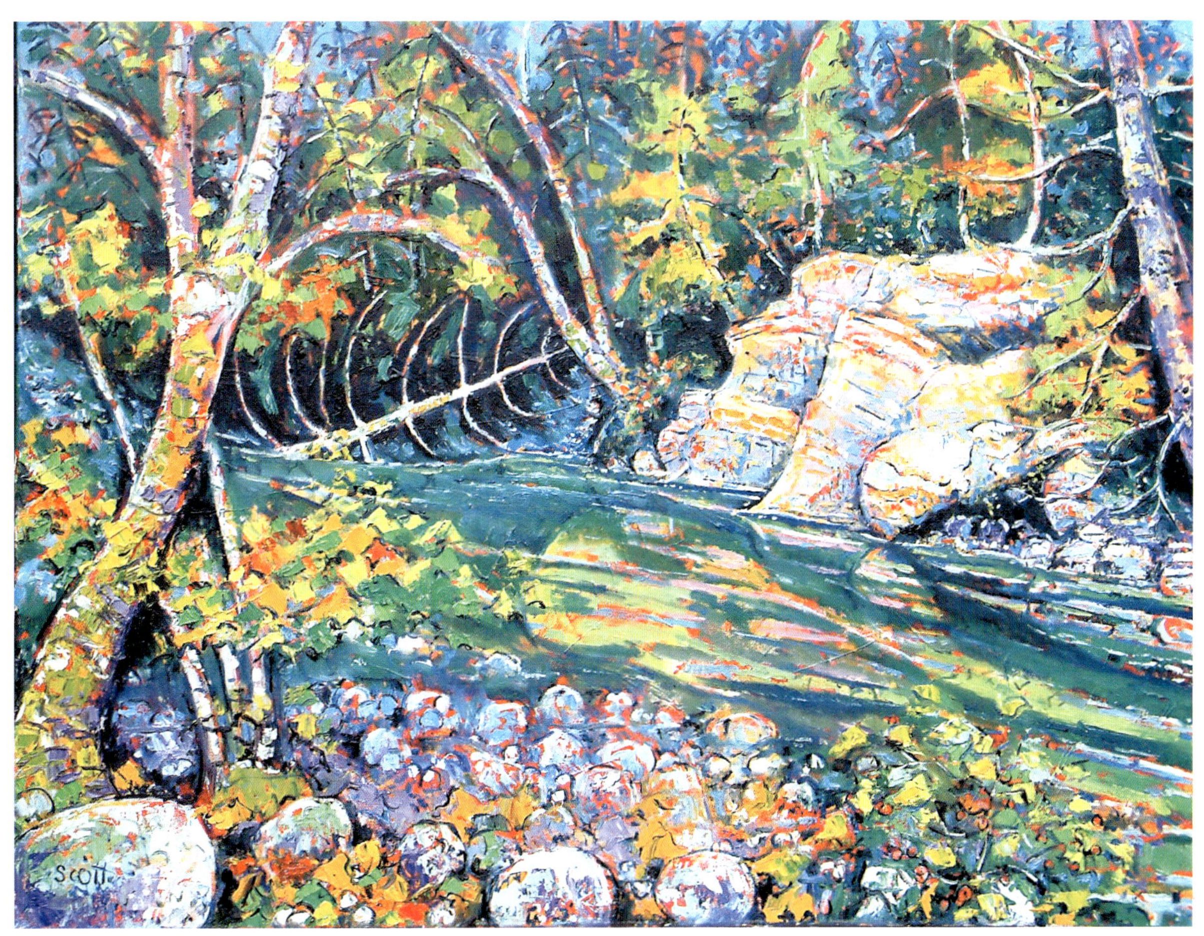

Oil on Canvas, 30 x 40 inches. "Puntledge Park"

Lions Gate Bridge

Long before the British Columbia Government took over the ferry service in the province, the 'Black Ball' Line was run by the Canadian Pacific Railway. These ferries ran between Nanaimo on Vancouver Island, and downtown Vancouver.

As a child, I rode these ferries back and forth to the Island. The most exciting part of the journey was sailing under the Lion's Gate Bridge. This formidable structure was built in 1936. It joins Vancouver to West Vancouver, crossing over the Strait of Georgia and is named for the "Lions" -twin mountain peaks that soar above the northern horizon. To me, the Lion's Gate Bridge was like the ultimate 'Lego' of the 40's and 50's.

The Guinness Family of Irish brewery fame built the bridge to further develop their interests in the British Properties in West Vancouver, vast stretches of land running up the side of the North Shore of Burrard Inlet. The sparkle of twinkle lights on the structure create a magic gateway to one of Canada's most beautiful cities.

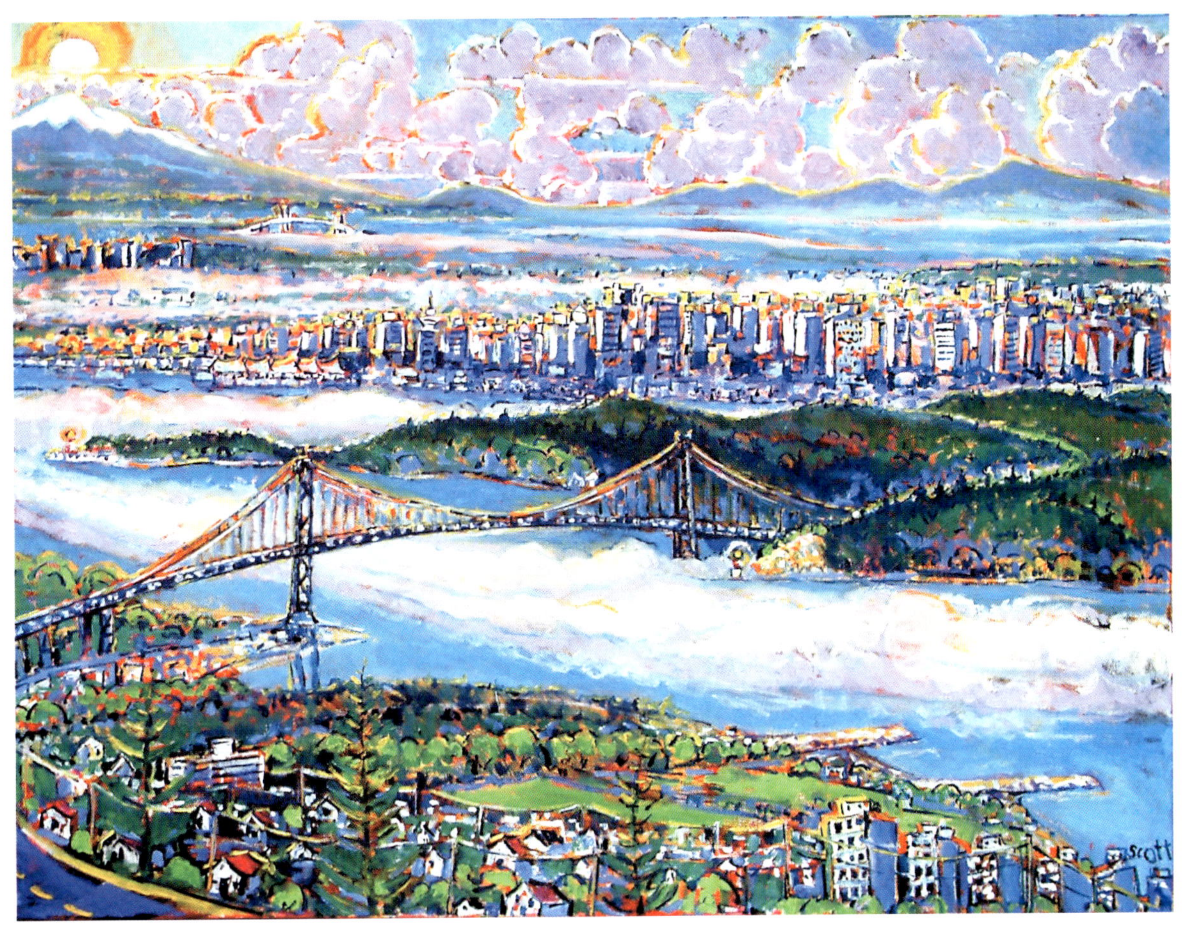

Oil on Canvas, 30 x 40 inches. "Sea Fog Lions Gate Bridge"

BC Packers #45

This boat, a treasure in Canadian History, now resides in Campbell River at the Maritime Heritage Center. For years she had been on display at the Maritime Museum in False Creek, Vancouver, but she 'came home' to Campbell River in 2002.

The BCP 45 had a crew of six. She was a BC product except for the oak gunnels. The hull is made of local Douglas fir with a superstructure of Red Cedar. Her length was 53 feet with a capacity of 5000 fish. Her home port was Quathiaski Cove across from Campbell River on Quadra Island. The old-timer is a big emotional 'hit' for locals since she was manned by local crews. She fished from Alaska to the mouth of the Fraser River, - salmon from May to November and herring in the spring.

BCP 45 was the Table Seiner pictured on the back of the Canadian five dollar bill in the 1960's. It was built in 1927 by Vancouver's Burrard Shipyards. When the five dollar bill with the BCP 45 was in circulation, it was the most common bill denomination used in Canada. Today, of course, the twenty dollar bill has taken its place!

The BC Packer 45 is reminiscent of the 'glory days' of fishing on the BC Coast.

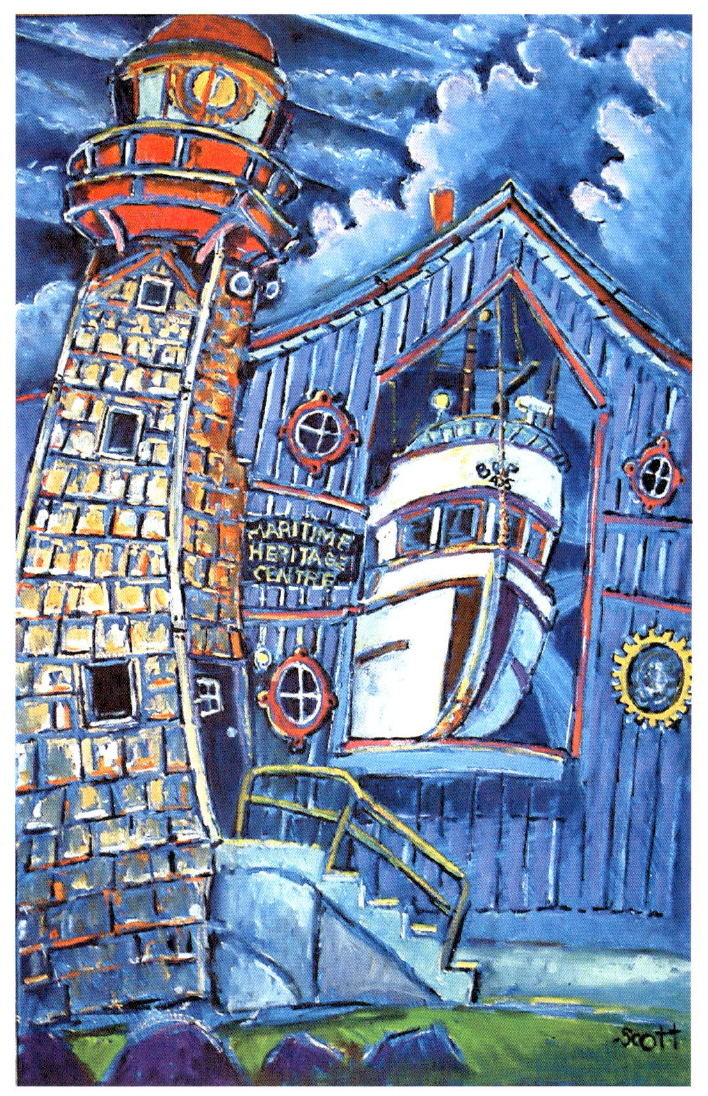

Oil on Canvas, 24 x 36 inches. "Heritage Lighthouse"

Quadra Island and Quathiaski Cove

Bodaga Y Quadra, an 18th century Spanish explorer, gave his name to Quadra Island, one of the largest of the Northern Gulf Islands of B.C. Quadra sailed his ships, called "Carabelas" from Spain around Cape Horne, and up the Westcoast of the Americas in some of the most treacherous waters in the world, a worthy testament to his seamanship. The British explorer Captain Vancouver joined forces with the Spanish and they jointly mapped the B.C coast looking for the Northwest passage to Asia.

One can find their routes not only from their journals but also by the names of the islands and inlets. For example, Cortez and Saturna are obviously of Spanish origin whereas Denman and Hornby are British names. The name Quathiaski came from the local First Nations who live at Cape Mudge. As soon as these explorers hit salt water and tidal action at Seymour Narrows they realized the Inside Passage would not lead to China!

Quathiaski Cove on Quadra with its Cannery Row, Post Office and General Store was the business center for what is now Campbell River. The Thulin family built the dock but the store didn't arrive until much later so early Campbell River pioneers had to row a boat across the water to do their shopping, quite a dangerous undertaking. Many stories have been told about harrowing experiences in fog banks, whirlpools, and southeasters!

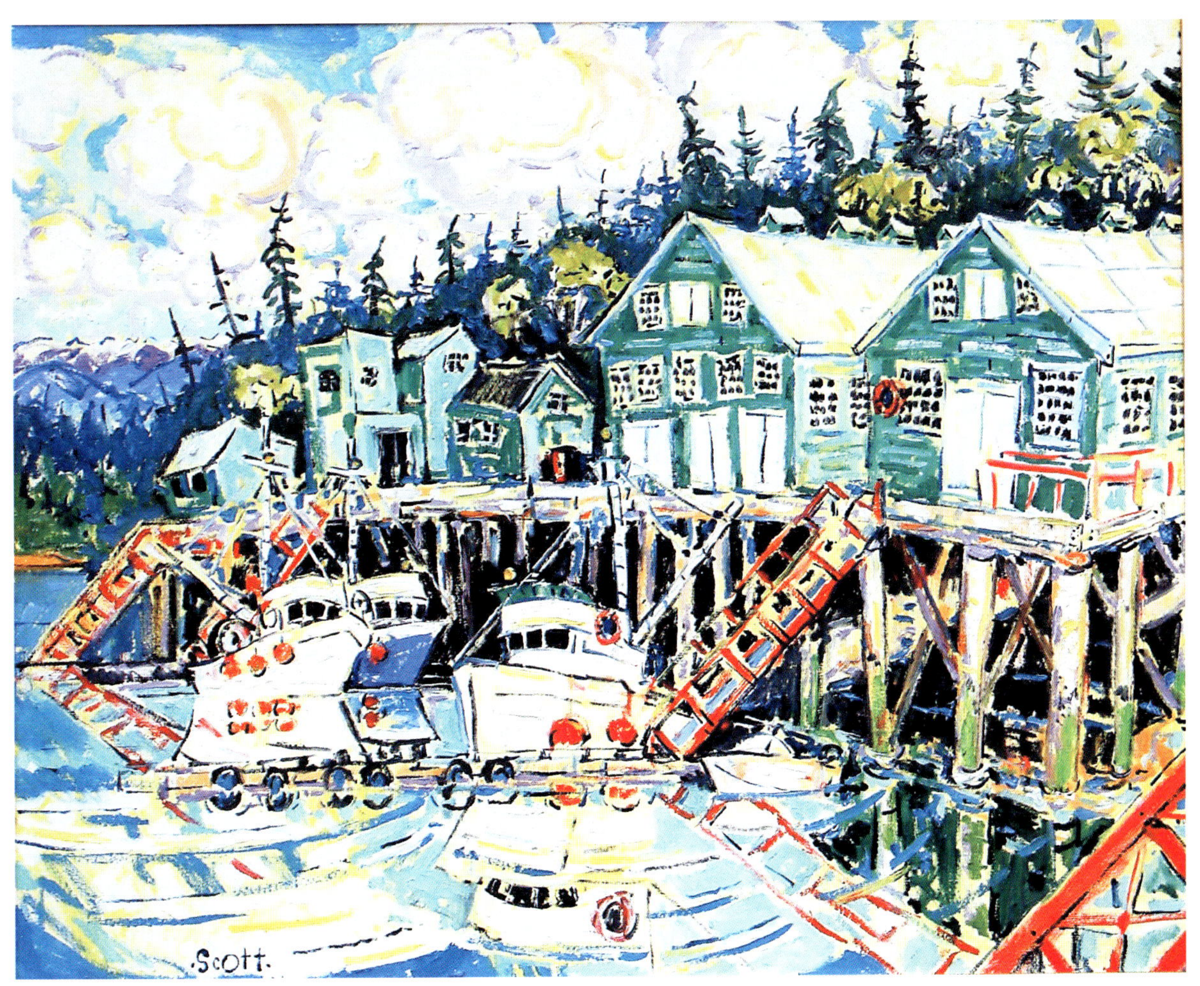

Oil on Panel, 24 x 30 inches. "Quathiaski Cove Cannery"

Salmon Canneries

At one time, there were 90 canneries on the BC Coast stretching all the way to Alaska. Since there was no refrigeration literally every salmon river run had to have a cannery in the vicinity. The fish had to be canned within three days or they would spoil.

A whole lifestyle grew up around the life cycle of the five species of Pacific Salmon. When the season began, a mass migration took place from the lower mainland as workers and their families left to work for the lucrative fishing industry. The union steamships dropped off people and cargo at all the logging and fishing camps up the coast.

Many fascinating stories have been written about this unique period in British Columbia's history. The early "gillnetters" operated with sails. Each cannery rented their fleet of sailing gillnetters and at the beginning of a fishing day one lone power boat would tow the whole fleet out to the fishing grounds.

Today each fish boat packs ice onboard, and some of the larger boats have their own refrigerators on board. The glory days of the canneries are finished, with most having rotted away in the damp Westcoast climate.

I love painting these relics, but only a very few of these treasures remain.

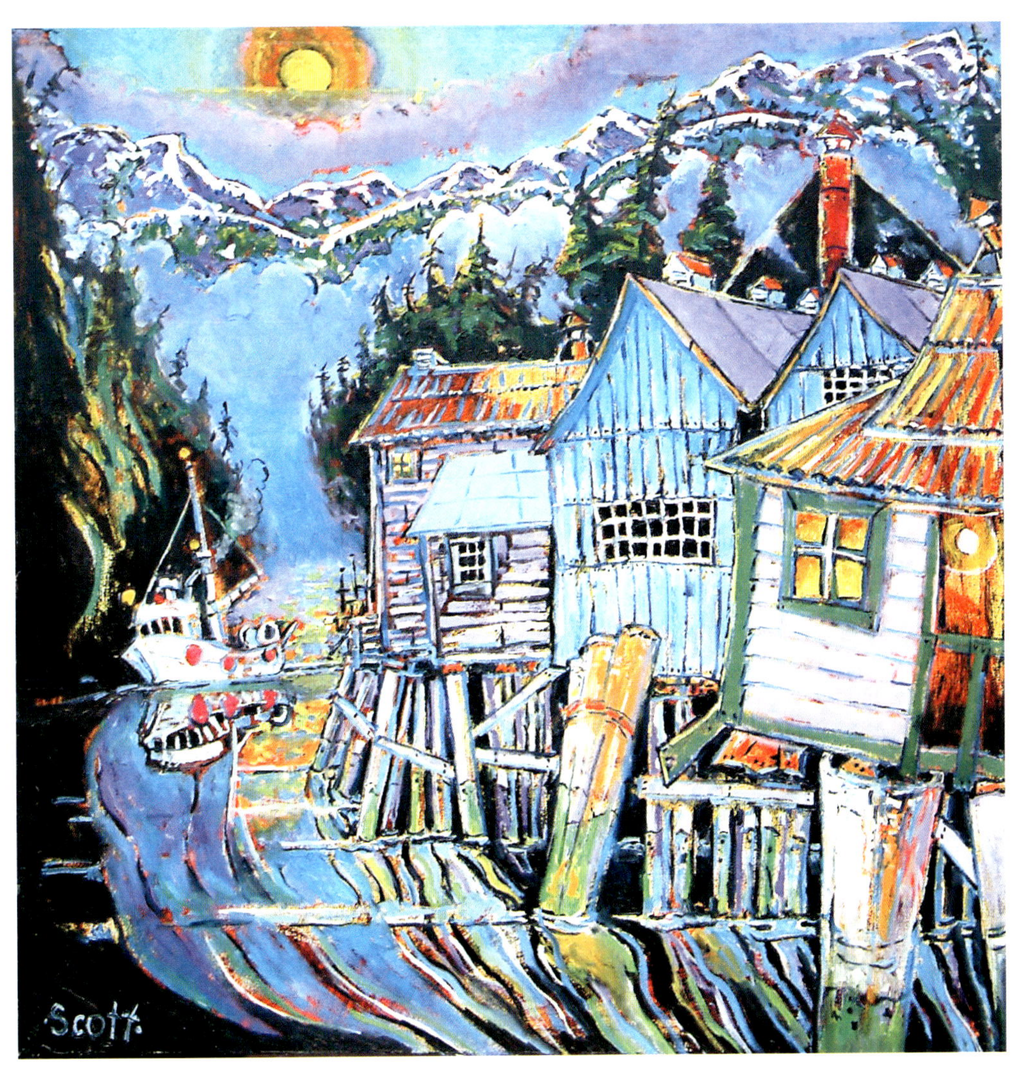

Oil on Canvas, 36 x 36 inches. "Light in Forest Cannery"

Herring Fleet

Once a year herring congregates on the beaches of coastal British Columbia to spawn. The females are laden with eggs that command a high price in Japan. The herring fishery is heavily regulated and the fisheries only last a week with several "openings".

It's an exciting time. For years I wanted to do some paintings of the event, however usually the boats were miles away. In 2002 I got lucky, the opening was in front of my studio in Union Bay! Seine boats with large nets, smaller crafts and packers all congregated on the schools of herring. The build up to the Opening was intense. Department of Fisheries boats went up and down Baynes Sound trying to predict where the best fishing locations would be. Float planes swooped down from the sky. Huge fish packers lumbered up the Sound, preparing for on-location processing. It was exhilarating, -an enormous amount of activity. Then the fleet disappears, like magic. It's all over in a matter of hours!

From an artist's point of view I think it's the emotional intensity of the "opening" that attracts my attention, - along with the incredible variety of vessels taking part. From sleek snub nosed steel hulled seine boats to long, wooden hulled old timers, the herring fleet presents itself as a myriad of bright colors and boats of every color and description.

After the opening, there's also a huge cash infusion to the many small fishing villages on the coast as the fishermen loaded with dollars head for port to quench their thirst.

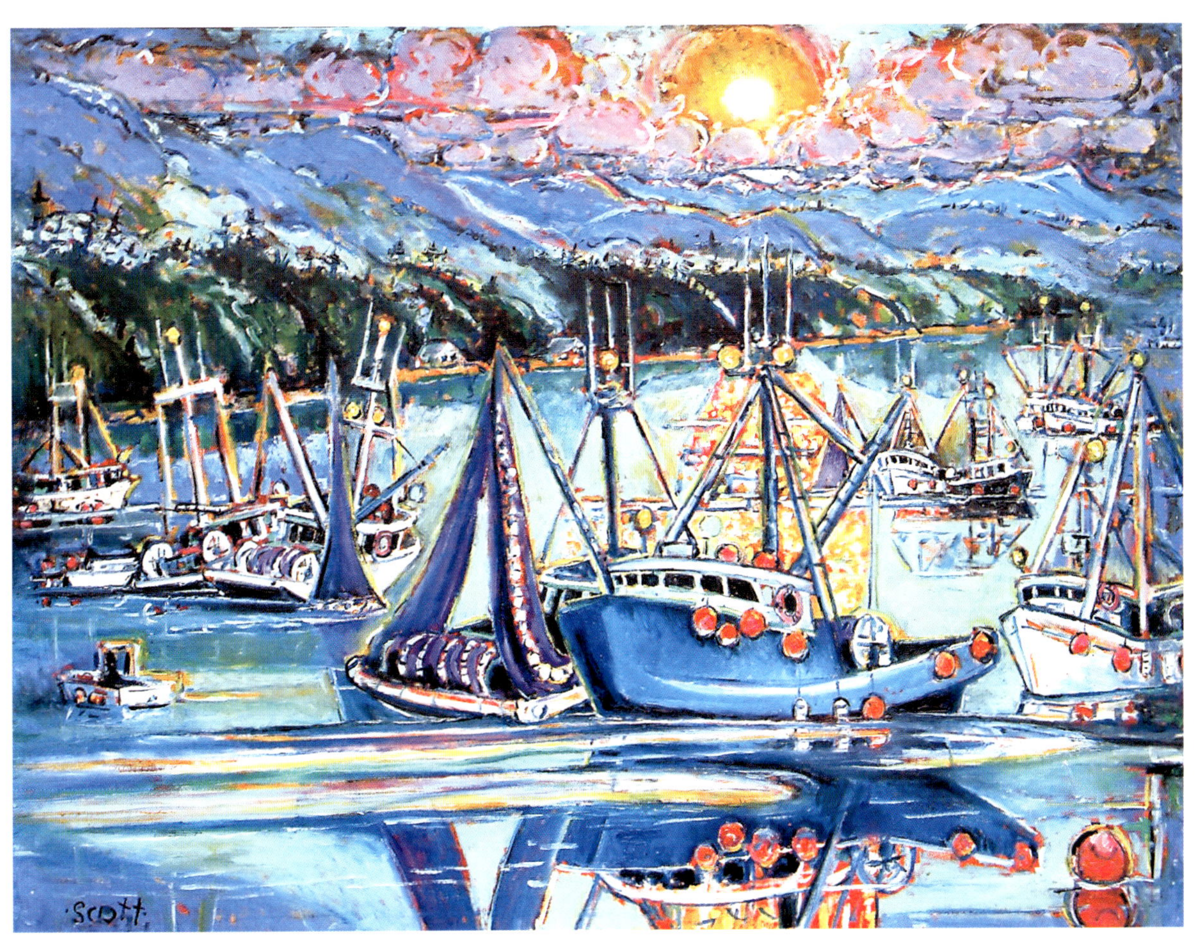

Oil on Canvas, 30 x 40 inches. "Herring Fleet Sunset"

Fishboats and the Northern Lights

The West Coast salmon boat is an artist's dream. The sweeping lines of the bow and stern are designed to withstand Pacific storms. The dramatic vertical poles on trollers are used to suspend steel lines anchored by cannon balls (huge lead weights) on which up to 35 lures are attached. All this is held together by a system of rigging which carries the eye on the diagonal. The horizontal lines of the dock and pilings are broken up by bright red bumpers. Overhead there are both the all important radar as well as powerful search lights to penetrate deadly sea fog.

Its interesting how ideas emerge from the act of painting. For many years I have observed the northern lights. I have seen this phenomena many times from my hot tub at my old studio in Union Bay as well as my many trips north teaching art in small northern communities for the Outreach Program at the Provincial Art School. I couldn't imagine how I could tackle the task of painting this amazing spectacle.

Suddenly there it was! The vertical movement of the fishing poles on the trollers reminded me of the glow of the northern lights and how they radiated up from the horizon. Their colors were subtle, with cool tints of green and yellow as well as mauve and pink glows. From a design perspective this worked well, -the movement of the poles accentuated the colors of the dramatic night sky and the Aurora Borealis.

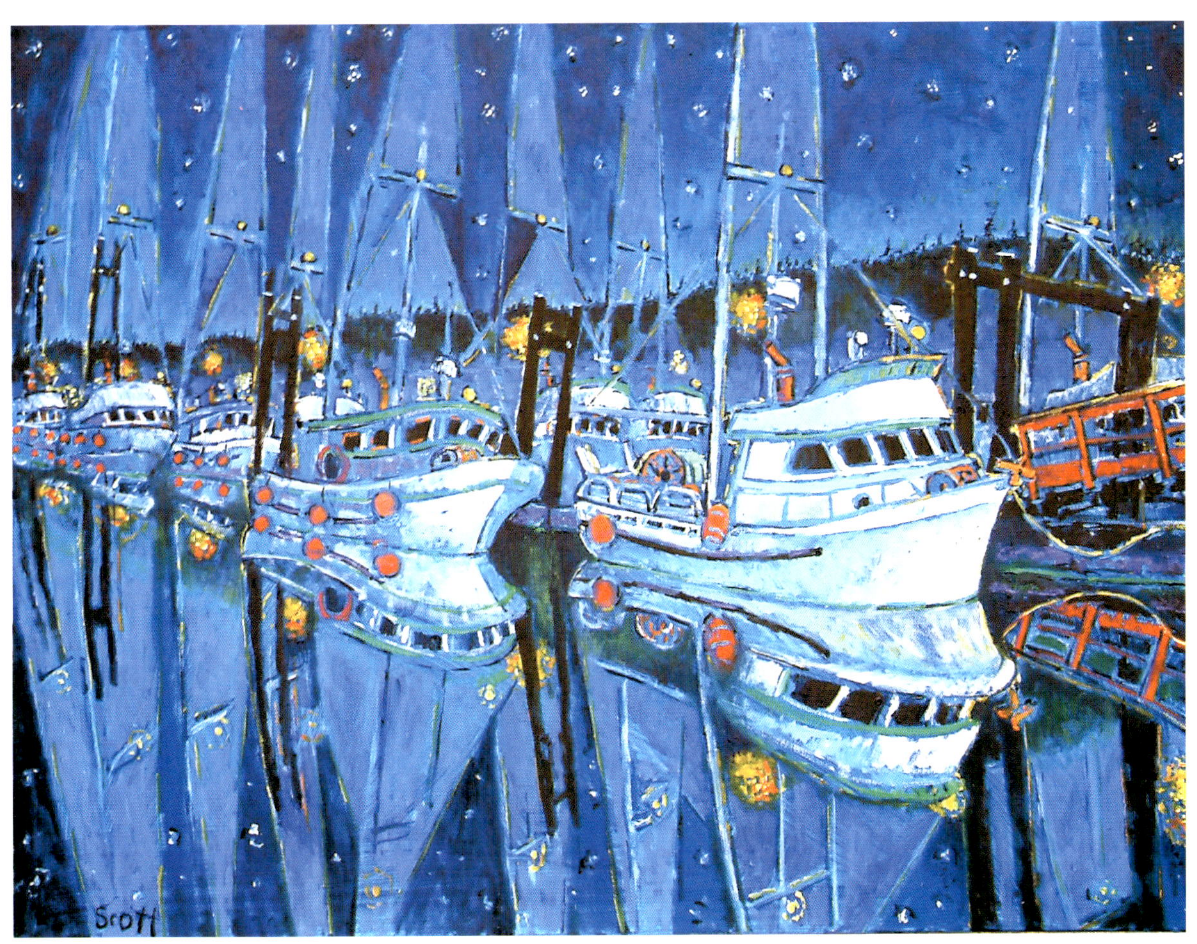

Oil on Canvas, 30 x 40 inches. "Fishboats Northern Lights"

Sandy and Des Kennedy's Garden

Des Kennedy is famous on the Coast, and indeed, across Canada, as a writer, broadcaster and expert on Westcoast gardening. He is the clear celebrity at Vancouver's Van Dusen Garden Show each year in June. Combining a great sense of humor and gardening expertise, -he draws huge crowds.

Sandy and Des Kennedy's home and garden on Denman Island is a magical place. The classic Westcoast home has lots of windows, cedar shake roofs, and steep gables to keep out the rain.

Like many 'back to the land' folk of the 60's and early 70's, they had lots of youthful energy but no money. Creativity was in order and recycling was the solution. The huge beams supporting the structure came from an old sawmill in Campbell River. Many hours of cutting shakes from cedar discarded by early loggers supplied roofing shakes and siding. The "Alaska Mill", a simple technology using a chain saw set-up allowed the young couple to mill trees from the property into useable building materials.

Each year during the Denman Home and Garden Tour, Sandy and Des patiently answer an enormous barrage of questions dealing with the incredible complexity of creating such a spectacular and diverse garden.

Their garden will host up to 1000 on any given tour weekend, and no visitor to this Island hideaway leaves disappointed.

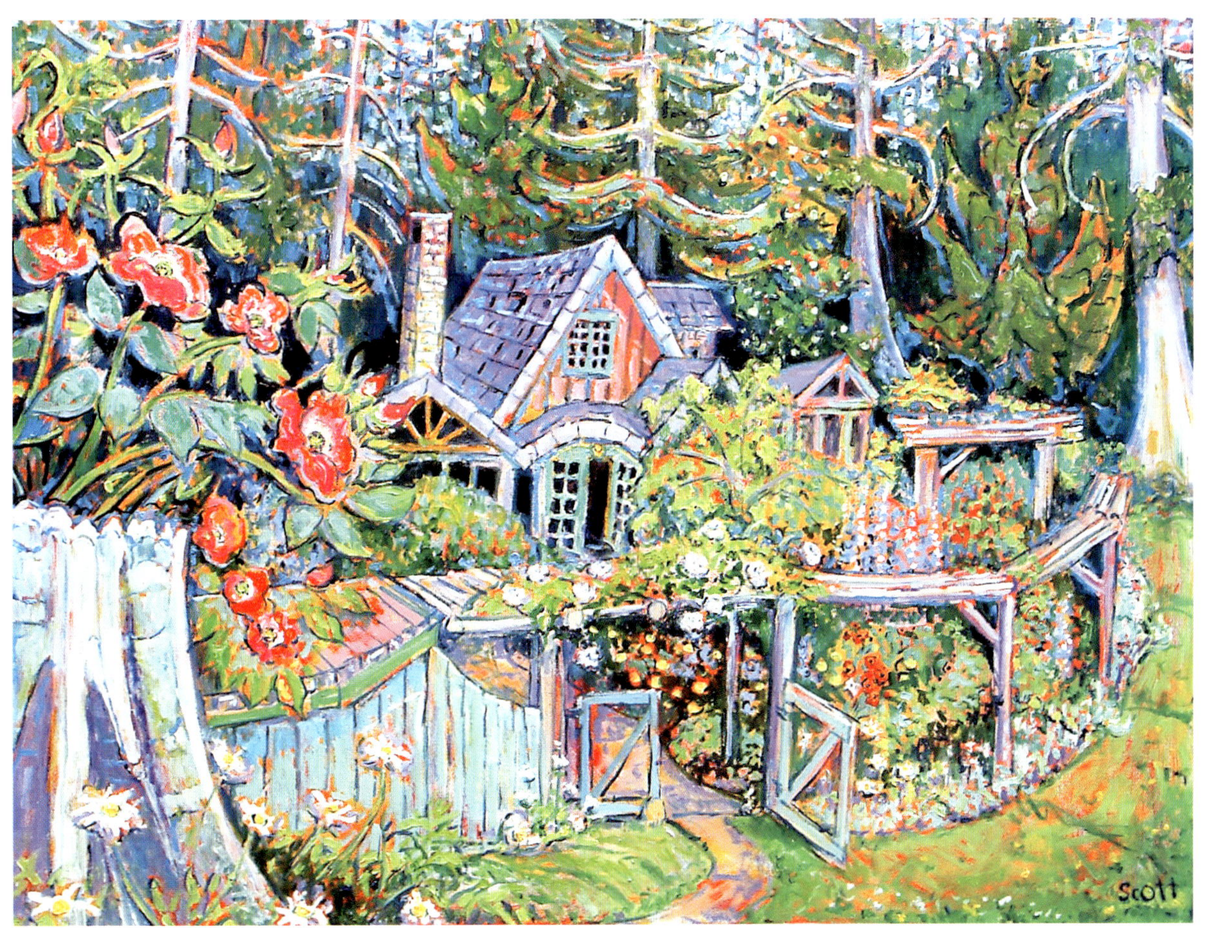

Oil on Canvas, 30 x 40 inches.

Western Red Cedar and Landscape

The Western Red Cedar tree was an integral part of Northwest Coast Native culture. From canoes to clothing, totem poles to long houses, the Red Cedar featured widely in native culture.

Red Cedar's natural characteristics made it ideally suited for Native use with primitive tools. The bark strips from the trees easily, and then could be further split into long fine lengths that were softened, dyed and woven into baskets and clothing. Bark could be harvested from a living tree over and over again without damaging the tree. The wood itself has a natural chemical makeup that makes it water resistant, an essential quality in the rainforest climate on Vancouver Island! Cedar is extremely lightweight compared to the Douglas Fir, another common BC native softwood. These two characteristics; water repulsion and lightness make old growth cedar a splendid candidate for roofing shingles, 'shakes' -as they are called in B.C.

Western Red Cedar allowed the great artistry of the Northwest Coast First Nations to achieve incredible sophistication. It is a wood that is easily carved into bowls and boxes, rattles and masks, (to name just a few items) and the skill and design that went into these items are well respected. The B.C. Museum of Anthropology at UBC, and many museums worldwide have wonderful examples of this spectacular art form.

Old growth cedars such as those in Cathedral Grove on the way to Port Alberni on Vancouver Island have attained heights of 200 feet and are 10 to 12 feet across at the trunk. Emily Car, British Columbia's preeminent artist was greatly inspired by the sweeping rhythms of these gentle giants.

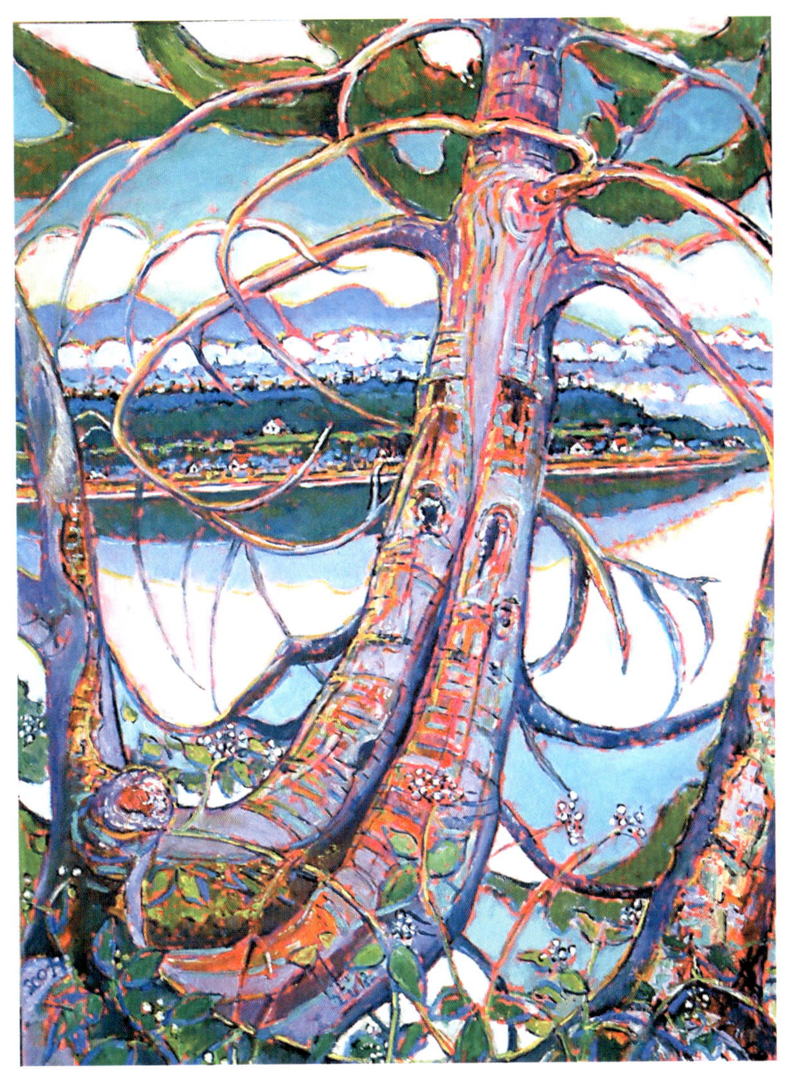

Oil on Canvas, 30 x 40 inches. "Red Cedar"

Snow Forms Mount Washington

In 1996 Mount Washington on Vancouver Island recorded a snow pack of 1000 centimetres or 30 feet of snow. Tourists complained to the management of the ski resort that there was too much snow! You had to ski up the mountains to get to the chair lifts, as they were covered in snow.

From an artists perspective, the mountain looked like a massive snow sculpture. The whole forest was buried under this bizarre snow fall which in turn was carved by high winds off the Pacific Ocean. I am an avid cross country skier and was enchanted by this phenomenon while on the mountain and back in the studio, completed a series of paintings called Snow Forms.

My imagination went wild producing a myriad of monster forms! Beautiful women in profile! Towering snow ghosts! With the backdrop of the sunset I could use a full spectrum of colors from west coast pinks to cool greens and blues.

The German philosopher Gotte wrote a thesis on color theory, based on the fact that snow under bright sun is so strong that it forces the eye to see blue or purple in the shadows. Today this is called simultaneous contrast. Scientists still cannot explain why the brain sees the opposite color.

However to a colorist this couldn't have been better. I saw fantastic curving organic forms illuminated with a shower of contrasting cool and warms colors. Magic!

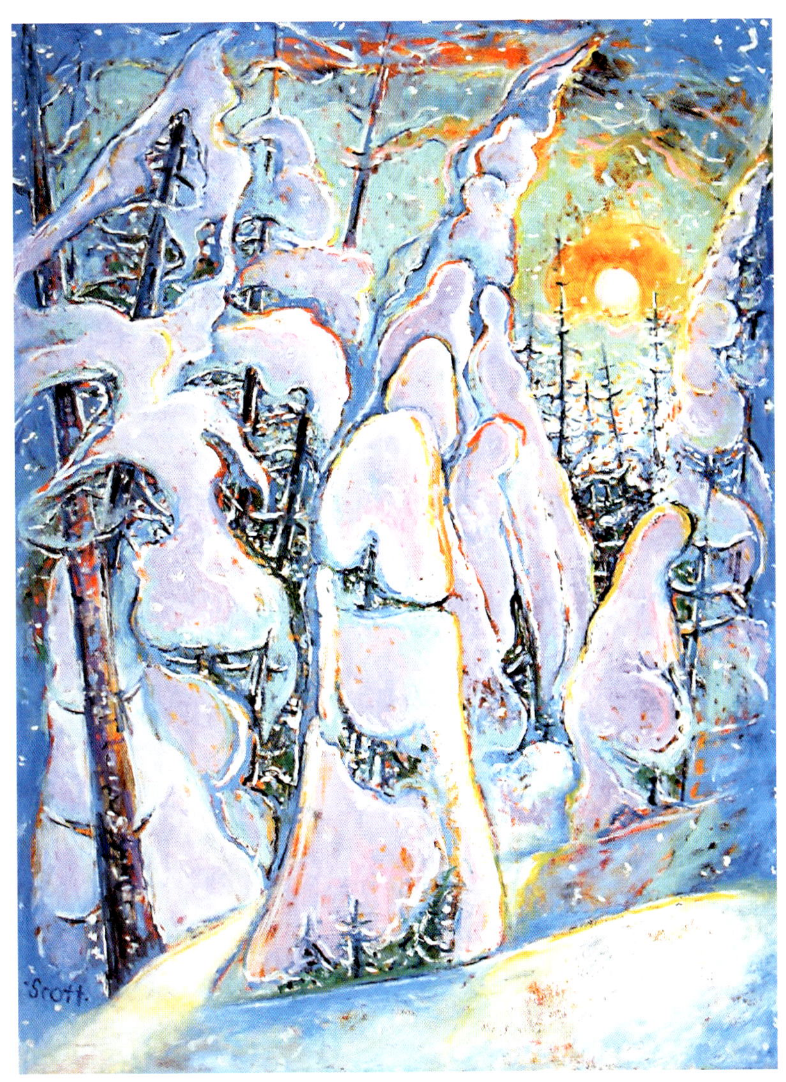

Oil on Canvas, 30 x 40 inches. "Snow Forms Sunset"

Dinghy Dock

Wherever sailing lessons are given there is a Dinghy Dock. This is where many kids have their first experiences with boating and sailing. Using only wind power requires skill and a sense of adventure. How do you manoeuvre out of the congested harbour area under sail alone? You have to know where the wind is coming from and, at the same time, you have to keep an eye on harbour traffic. This is exciting stuff for youngsters and there's usually lots of yelling going on. No amount of land based teaching can totally prepare even an adult for dinghy sailing. When you're near a dinghy dock, emotions run high!

Life jackets are mandatory as many a kid has been dumped in the salt chuck as wind suddenly shifted. Sailing is wonderfully simple but requires intense concentration and a fierce discipline alien to most children. However once they experience the rush of the close-hulled pull of the sails, and can maneuver as close as possible to the direction of the wind without tacking, they're hooked! They are ready to enjoy the beam reach allowing the sail to billow out in maneuvers downwind at a leisurely pace.

On the coast you can always expect an evening off shore breeze to bring you home if you are becalmed. The cold current from Alaska is roughly 37 degrees Celsius year-round so the land heats up through the day. Then later in the day, there comes a rush of the warm to cold creating this predictable evening wind, -to the relief of many a becalmed sailor.

If you are observant you might sail through an evening bite. When the salmon attack the herring for one last feed before dark, the seabirds become very active. They feed on the herring as they are driven to the surface by the predatory salmon. All that is required is a fishing rod and a buzz bomb, a lure that simulates a wounded herring, -easy prey for a hungry Coho salmon. Fresh salmon on the barbecue is a spectacular finish to a day at sea!

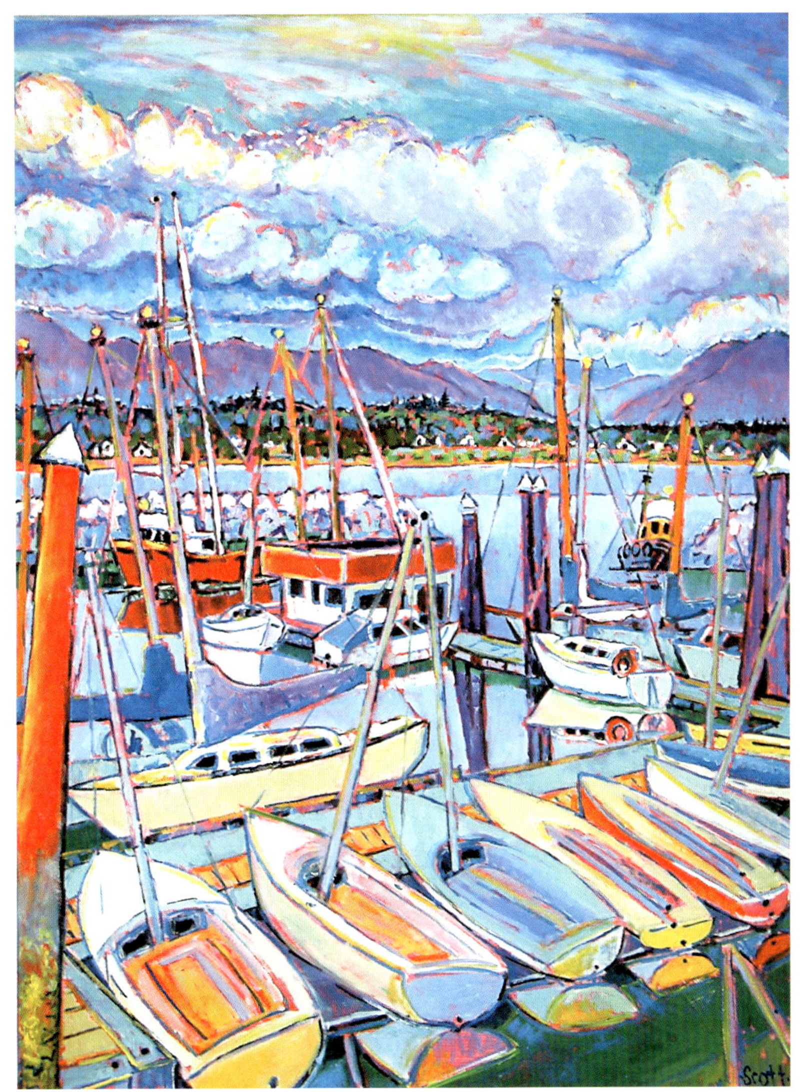

Oil on Canvas, 30 x 40 inches.

Boating on the Coast of B.C.

Fisherman spend a lot of time around government wharves working on their boats, drinking beer and swapping stories. My favorite story is about sport fishing in Black Fish Sound at the north end of Vancouver Island. My older brother was fishing with Mike, -owner of Hick's Lodge near Malcolm Island. Fishing alongside them was a husband and wife in a small, open boat.

When the tide comes up from the south end of Vancouver Island and meets the incoming tide down from the north Pacific side, this conflict of waters can create whirlpools with devastating severity. Sure enough, the small sports boat got caught in a whirlpool and was suddenly capsized! Hick's 100 horsepower Mercury outboard motor sprang to life as he headed to try to save the couple.

They managed to pull the husband aboard but were unable to find the wife. My brother tells the story that just then a whirlpool opened up and he saw a hand reach up out of the watery depths. It was the wife! He managed to quickly grasp her hand firmly and yank her aboard!

To his surprise and great amazement, in her other hand, in a firm grip, was her purse!

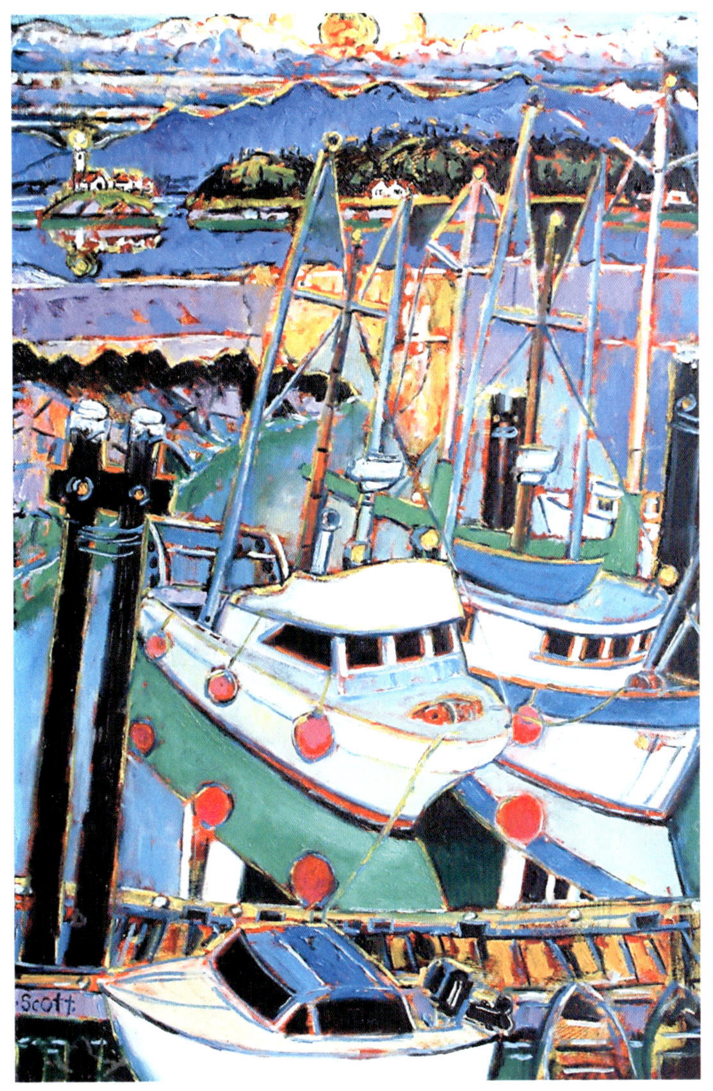

Oil on Canvas, 60 x 40 inches.

The Red Boat, Cortez Island

I have painted fish boats and sail boats up and down the coast of British Columbia and have found the brightest colored ones are on Cortez Island across from Campbell River. I have developed a theory that the closer you get to where marijuana is grown, the brighter the colors of the boats in the harbor. My other favorite painting location for brightly colored boats is Hornby Island. I haven't told the authorities my theory, -but I think they may already know.

Marijuana is the biggest agricultural cash crop in the Province of B.C. However, being an illegal business, exhaustive measures are used to keep the crop hidden away in the hills and valleys of the Gulf Islands. These plantings require constant attention, heavy watering and fertilizing along with vigilant guard duty. Emotions run high and tension abounds in the fall when the crop is ready to harvest!

A helicopter full of police can swoop out of the sky and a year of extremely hard work can disappear in a hastily assembled bonfire. Alternately, thieves can also invade the fields and steal the crop. This the reason most "grow-ops" are indoors now, using hydroponics technology and strong lighting rather than chance the loss of an outdoor crop.

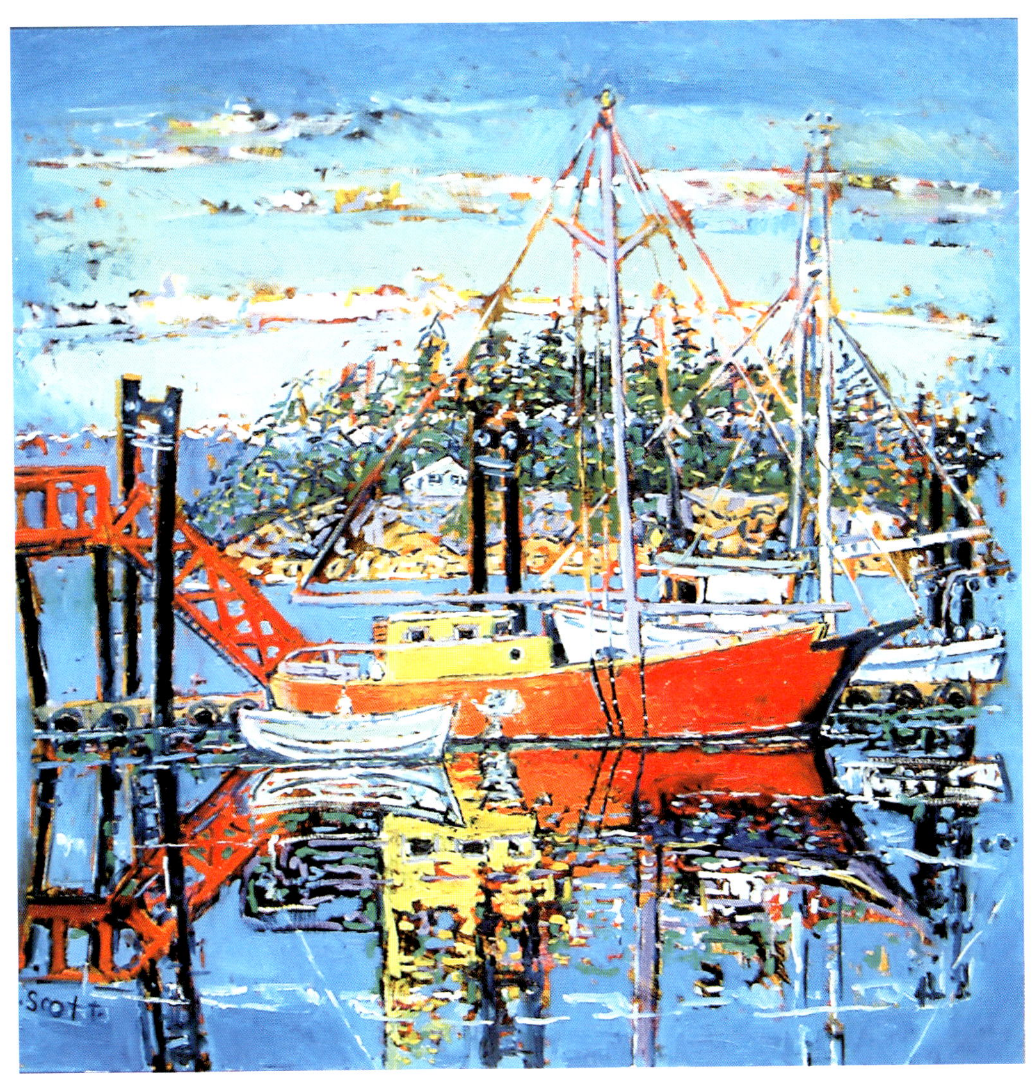

Oil on Canvas, 36 x 36 inches.

Union Bay and the Old Island Highway

In the past, Union Bay was the tide water shipping port for Cumberland Coal, and the massive coal slag heap to the north of the town is a testament to its size and importance. Huge coal seams existed under the ancient strata of Vancouver Island, and actually only a small amount was ever mined. Today the methane gas deposits that caused the devastating mine explosions in the early days are being explored and developed. The coal port is long gone.

Spring is a wonderful time to be an outdoor artist, or as the French call it "plein air" painting. There is nothing more inspiring than to connect on canvas with the textures and colors of springtime on the West Coast after a gloomy winter. Van Gogh thought nature was a study of textures, -that artists should imitate those textures with the brush stroke, -either flat, round or pointed to achieve the effect.

In this particular scene on the Old Island Highway, I'm contrasting the colours of the spring garden with the snow fields of the Coast mountains across the Strait of Georgia. The waterway is busy with tug boats, sail boats and ocean going freighters.

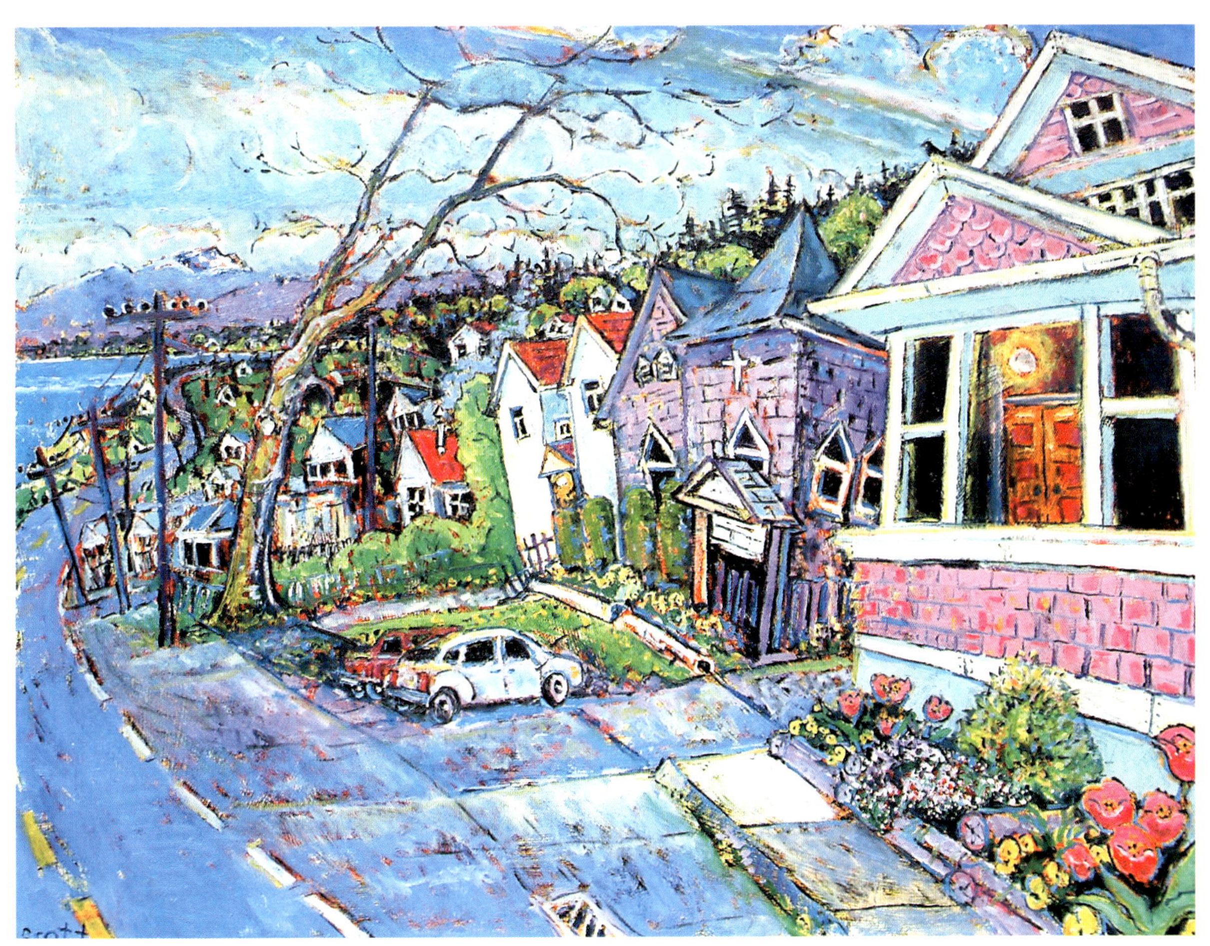

Oil on Canvas, 30 x 40 inches. "Union Bay"

'57 Plymouth

The ' 57 Plymouth, like the Chevys and Cadillacs were classic icons of the 1950's. The sweeping tail fins and outrageous colors were symbolic of the exuberance of the post war years. The shapes of cars went from the soft rounded practical forms of the 1940's to the wild sharp-edged chrome beauties of the 50's.

On this old Plymouth, the four inch thick layer of moss caught and held my attention. This is so indicative of the rainforest on Vancouver Island. When the light illuminates the forest, it comes alive with rich colors and intricate textures that make an artist's imagination fly! This is one bonus of working on location. The forest is damp and cold but when the light breaks through the forest canopy "magic is afoot."

One of the reasons I prefer painting derelicts in the bush rather than mint show cars is the endless variety they offer me. Wrecked vehicles are an expression of life, -they have their wrinkles, bumps and rust. I often speculate that their history is like that of old houses. They all have a story to tell.

I find it interesting to watch a person's reaction to the paintings. They either have an instant emotional response or nothing. If they connect with the old cars, they'll have a story to tell. Always, it's about the family first car. Most families didn't own a car until the 1950's. Those first vehicles were a big deal! Today everyone has a car, -they're our symbol of freedom. But the question might be asked, are our modern cars a match for those of the fabulous 50's?

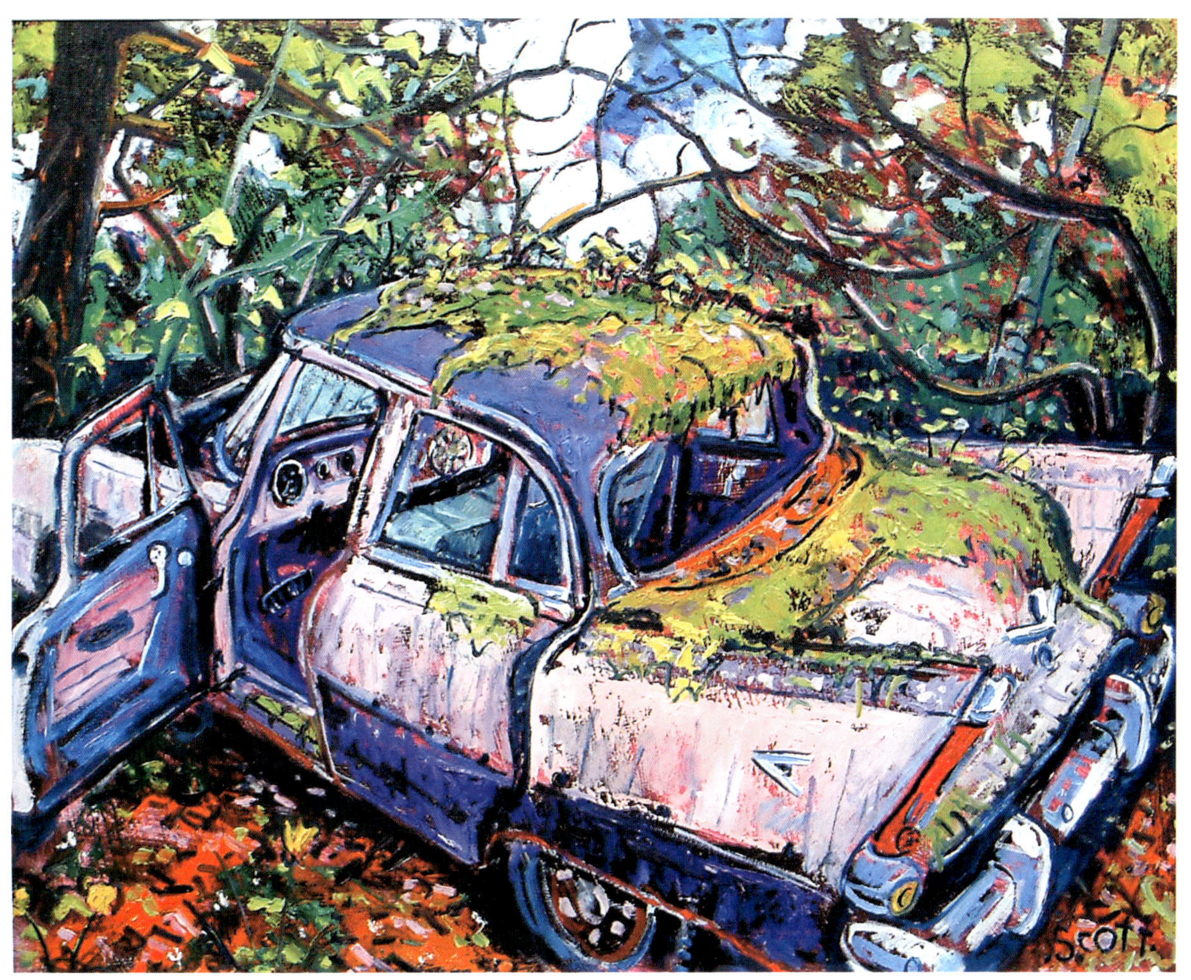

Oil on Panel, 24 x 30 inches. "End of the Road"

Haig-Brown House, Campbell River

A tourist from Campbell River was shopping at a fly-fishing outfitter while visiting London, England. He happened to mention he was from Campbell River, British Columbia. Business came to a halt as the visitor was instantly surrounded by curious shoppers wanting to know about Haig-Brown and Campbell River's famous fishing.

This story illustrates the world wide fame of Roderick Haig-Brown. Haig-Brown was known in Campbell River as the District Magistrate more than for the publication of his books. Not everyone was fascinated by trout fishing and especially fly-fishing which originated in England. Fooling a trout or salmon with various kinds of feathers and hair on a hook was no easy matter. It remains both an art and a science.

Rod and his wife, Anne Elmore, lived in Campbell River all their lives, raising a large family in a spectacular home on the river.

I was an avid fisherman before turning all my energy to oil painting. I was fascinated by Haig-Brown's books and the descriptions of the energy and diversity of the different seasons on Vancouver Island rivers. To be able to read an expertly written book on a river such as the Quinsam or the Campbell, and then to be able to go there and actually experience some of the action first hand was a thrill to me. Although I don't fish the rivers as much as I'd like to anymore, I still spend many happy hours on location painting their colours and textures.

Haig-Brown house is now a Heritage site, and operates as a Bed and Breakfast. Visitors can tour the library, house, and gardens along the bank of his much beloved Campbell River.

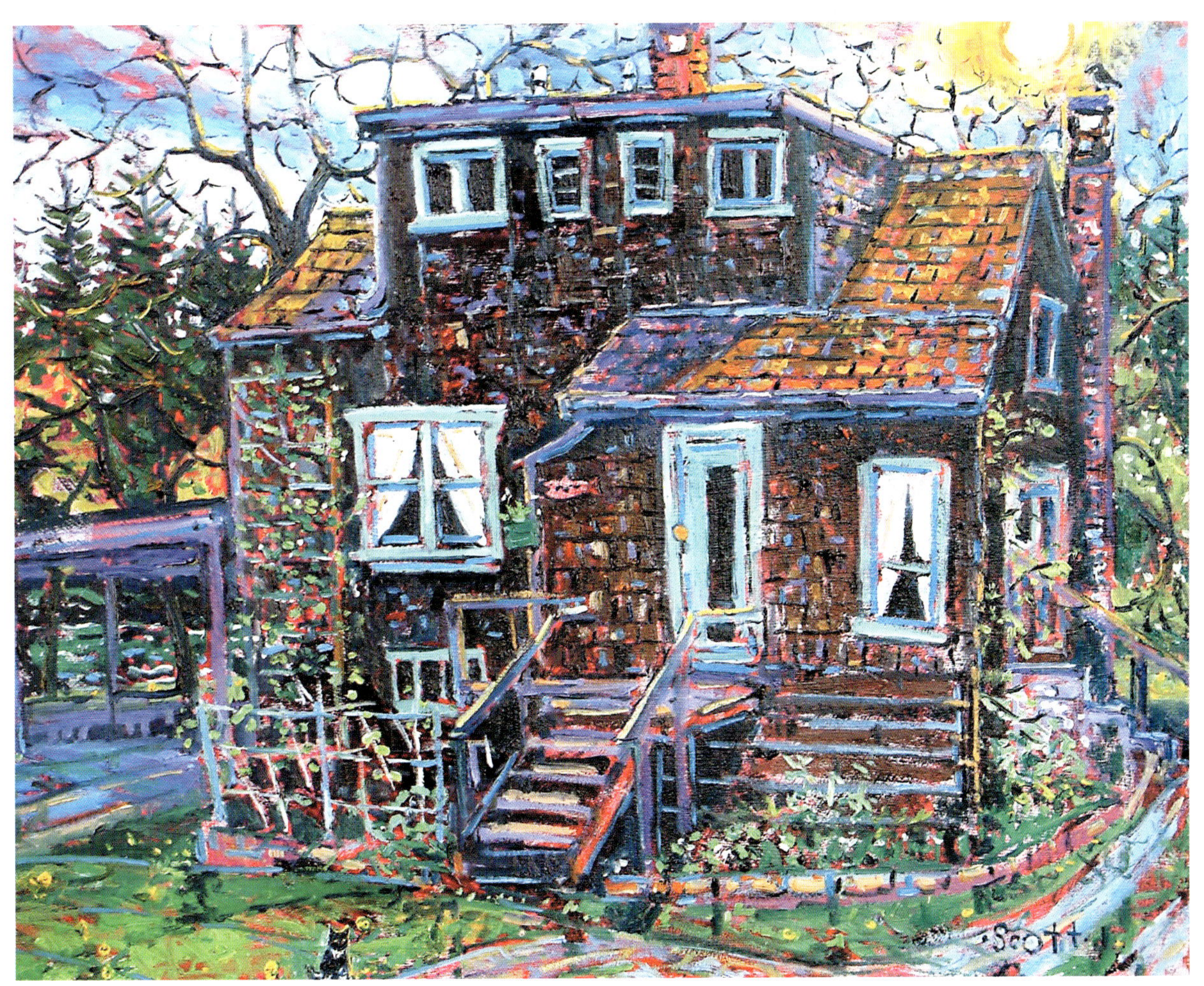

Oil on Panel, 24 x 30 inches. "Haig Brown House"

View from Painter's Lodge

Campbell River on Vancouver Island boasts of its exclusive "Tyee Club."

Tyee is the First Nations name for a large salmon. A fisherman must catch and land a 30 pound or larger Spring Salmon from a row boat in the "Tyee Pool" -a small area of water off the mouth of the Campbell to be a member of this prestigious club. No natural bait is allowed and only an artificial "plug" or "spoon" lure can be used. The rules for the tackle are complicated, and the competition is fierce.

One can only imagine the battle with so large a fish. They are quite literally capable of towing a small row boat around the tidal rips for hours. To row, year after year, trying to capture one of these magnificent fish requires extreme patience and determination.

Vancouver Island offers year round sports fishing, especially Salmon and Winter Steelhead, which are Trout that spend most of their lives in the ocean. Ed and June Painter built their lodge to serve this demand. One of my favorite fishing stories involves their son Joe Painter, many years later. He was guiding a family member visiting from England on a fishing trip. The visiting Brit caught a large salmon, but when they got it into the boat, they were surprised to see another fishing line running from the fish's mouth back into the water. Sure enough. They patiently pulled the line in -complete with another wonderful fishing rod and reel. That salmon had obviously taken the bait before, and the rod and reel too!

Many Hollywood stars came north to enjoy not only the fishing but Painters Lodge and spectacular scenery of Seymour Narrows. In the early days Bob Hope, Bing Crosby, and John Wayne made the Lodge the fishing destination of choice for Hollywood!

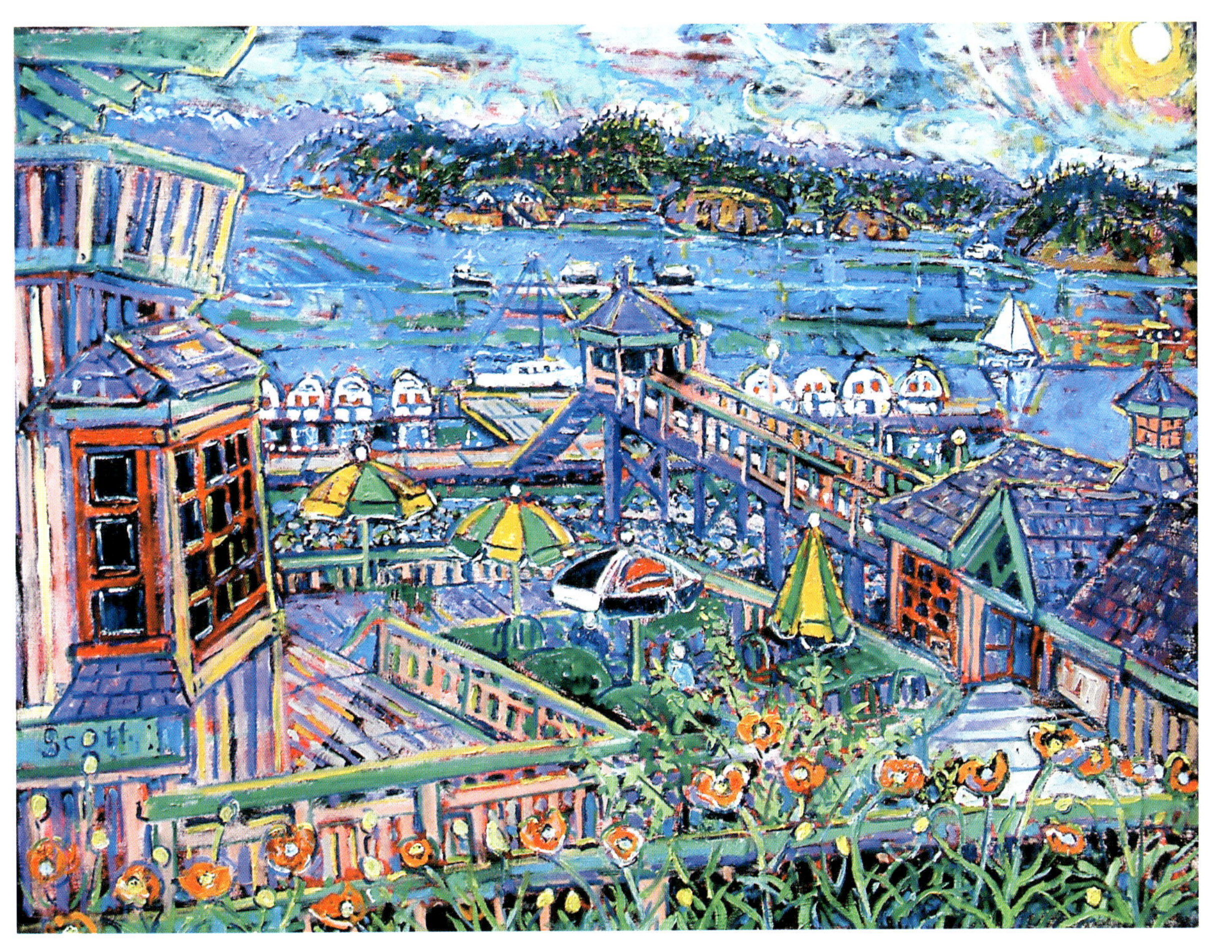

Oil on Canvas, 30 x 40 inches. "Vista Painter's Lodge"

Hornby Lookout

Since the 1960's, my family and I have summered on Hornby Island. I built my summer studio there in 1984. Every summer I would do an art show at the Hornby Hall, and to my great delight, (and often amazement) , Jack Shadbolt would always show up to 'critique' my new works. Years later, I found out that my father, Ralph, would simply phone up Mr. Shadbolt and ask him to look at my work. I was, and still remain, a great fan of the Artist, who was an 'icon' of Westcoast painting. I invited Jack to come to Cumberland to paint. I had always admired his paintings of Vancouver in the 1940's and 50's. Unfortunately, he had to decline my offer, -he was on a run with his work, and couldn't stop.

My favorite Shadbolt story was about when he visited Emily Carr's Studio in Victoria in the late 1930's. Emily apparently offered him a choice of either an art book or an original painting as a souvenir of his visit. Jack, much to his later amusement and perhaps disappointment, choose the art book over the painting!

Jack Shadbolt, together with Charles H. Scott, and other colleagues from the Vancouver School of Art loved Hornby Island and brought many aspiring art students to the studio on Tribune Bay to paint. It was the beginning of Hornby's illustrious reputation as perhaps the most artistic of any in the Gulf Islands.

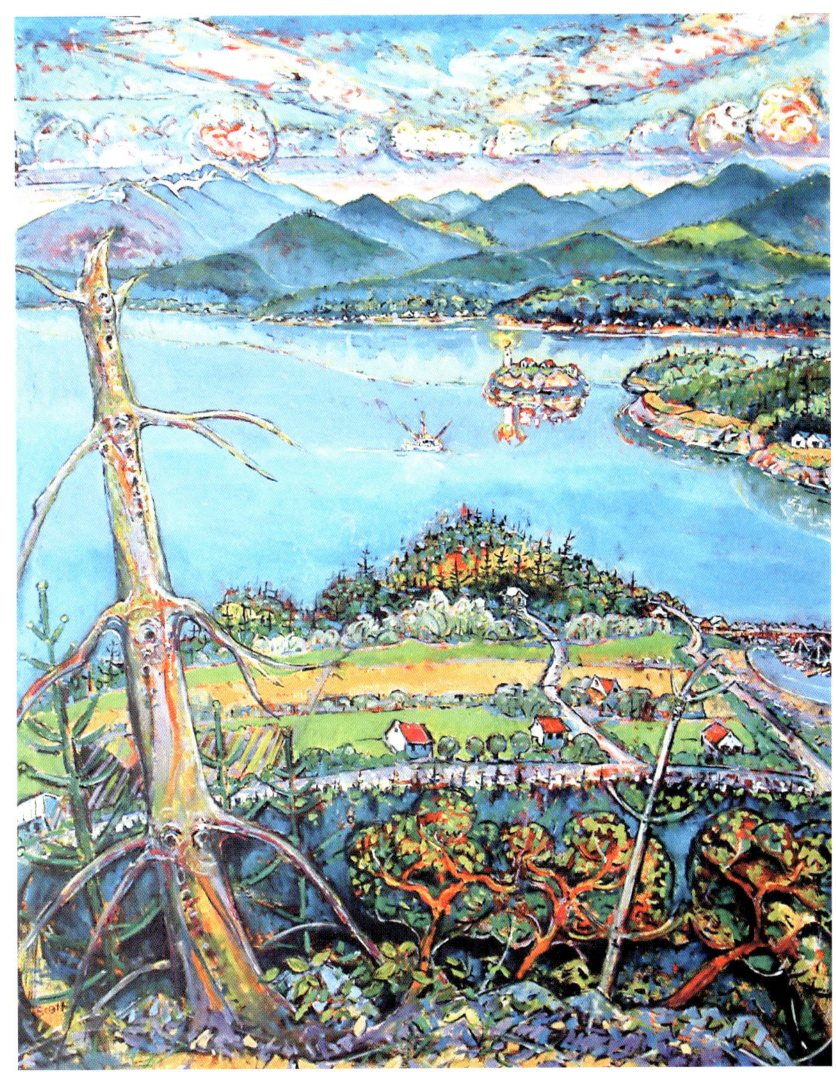

Oil on Canvas, 60 X 40 inches.

"Arbutus" The Knotty Lady Tree

The rainforest of British Columbia grows right to the edge of cliff faces lining the Strait of Georgia. This is the biological 'niche' where Arbutus grow, their trunks and branches extending out from precarious perches. The vibrant red/orange of this unique tree is in stark contrast to the green, blue and grey of the evergreen landscape, and Arbutus trees have long caught artists' attention. When you see these flame-like colors flashing on the edge of an otherwise dark and foreboding forest, you know you are on the Westcoast of Canada.

I did a showing of my Arbutus paintings and a young girl from Victoria took me aside to share a story. "Did you know what the kids in Victoria call the Arbutus trees?" she asked. She then informed me that "We call it the 'knotty lady tree' because she strips and streaks!" Arbutus wood has a smooth surface very much like human skin as it emerges 'stripped' from its bark. The tree form can be very dramatic as they drape themselves from the front of rugged cliff faces.

I prefer to paint Arbutus trees in the Gulf Islands either from Hornby or Cortez Island. The reasons are twofold: their trees there are very old, - up to 200 years, and these two particular Islands provide dramatic landscape backdrops to the trees themselves. In the background, I've painted stylized cloud forms, snow-capped mountains and chains of islands with summer cottages perched like birds on the rugged waterfront.

The scale is important. The tree form dominates the foreground and the branches break up the space. This allows for smaller pictures within the larger 'picture frame'. Since the smaller 'windows' are enclosed, this pulls them forward creating an interesting dialogue in the work.

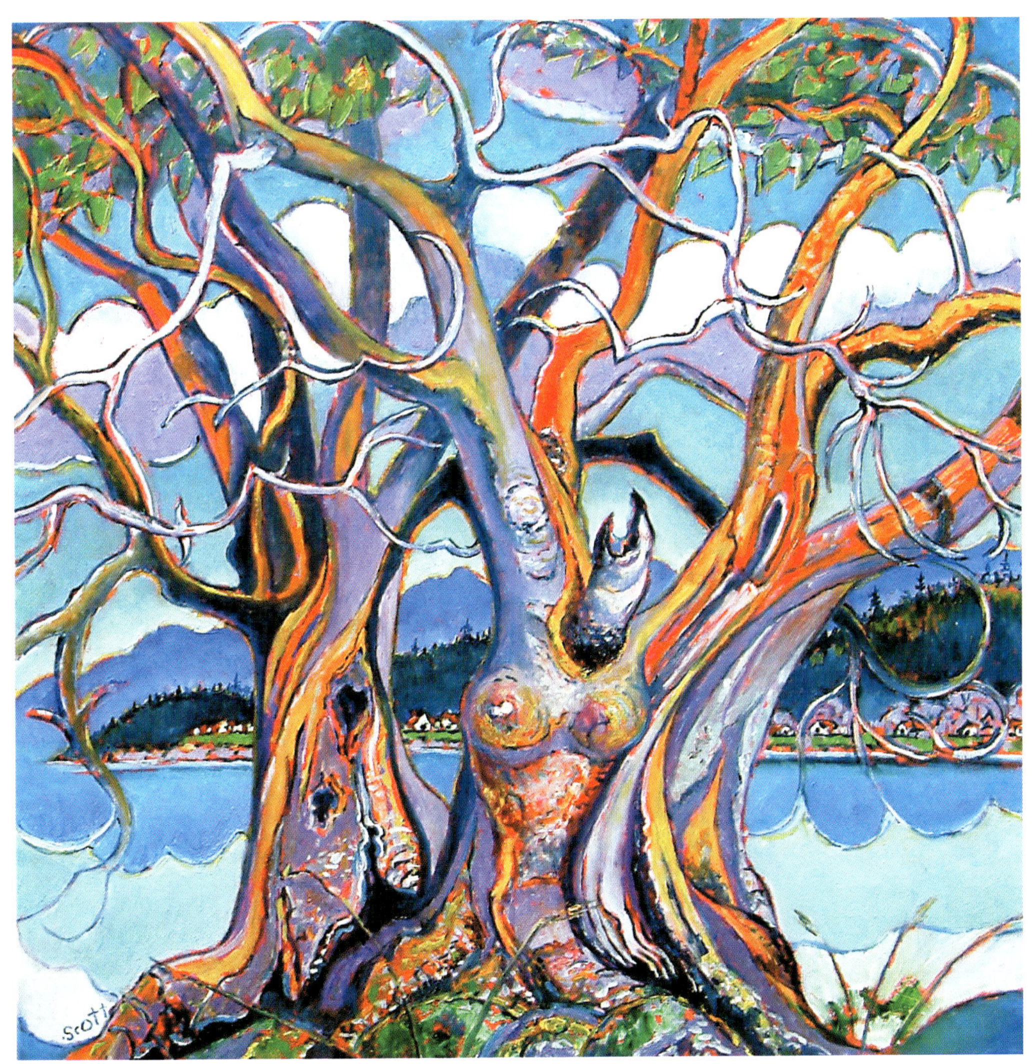

Oil on Canvas, 36 x 36 inches.

Filberg Lodge, Comox

Robert Filberg's name graces many public buildings in the Comox Valley. However, the largest portion of the family fortune originated with his wife's family, the McCormicks and Comox Logging Company.

Bob Filberg, eventually O.B.E., - was a visionary, and his Lodge in Comox is an expression of his unique personality. He firmly believed in the rights of the common worker. He is fondly remembered in Comox as buying up all available private shares that were for sale at the Comox golf course, and in turn donating them back to the Course, -but on the firm condition that the greens always remain open to the public. During the Great Depression, the American expatriate engineer kept his skilled building crews together by employing them to work on his waterfront acreage in Comox.

The steep gabled roof and massive stone chimneys have a individualistic appeal. His grand-daughter remembers wonderful mornings with her Granddad, playing cards in the breakfast nook overlooking the beautiful Comox Bay. It is the woodwork inside that makes the building outstanding. Local wood from the both the Island mountain tops (notably Yellow Cedar) to the valley bottoms (Red Cedar and Douglas Fir) have been used extensively in the Lodge. The interior wood finishing is spectacular.

These local woods have their own place in B.C. history. 'Doug' Fir is the hardest of the softwoods, and straight grained fir is heavy and strong. It was the wood of choice for beams and posts in large scale construction. Early sailing ships came to the coast to harvest Douglas fir spars for the rigging on Barques and Brigantines. These ancient sailing ships had to withstand fearsome Pacific gales, -when only the best B.C. timber would do.

Filberg Lodge will always have a special place in the hearts of Comox residents, -and I enjoy the times in the Lodge when I exhibit paintings there.

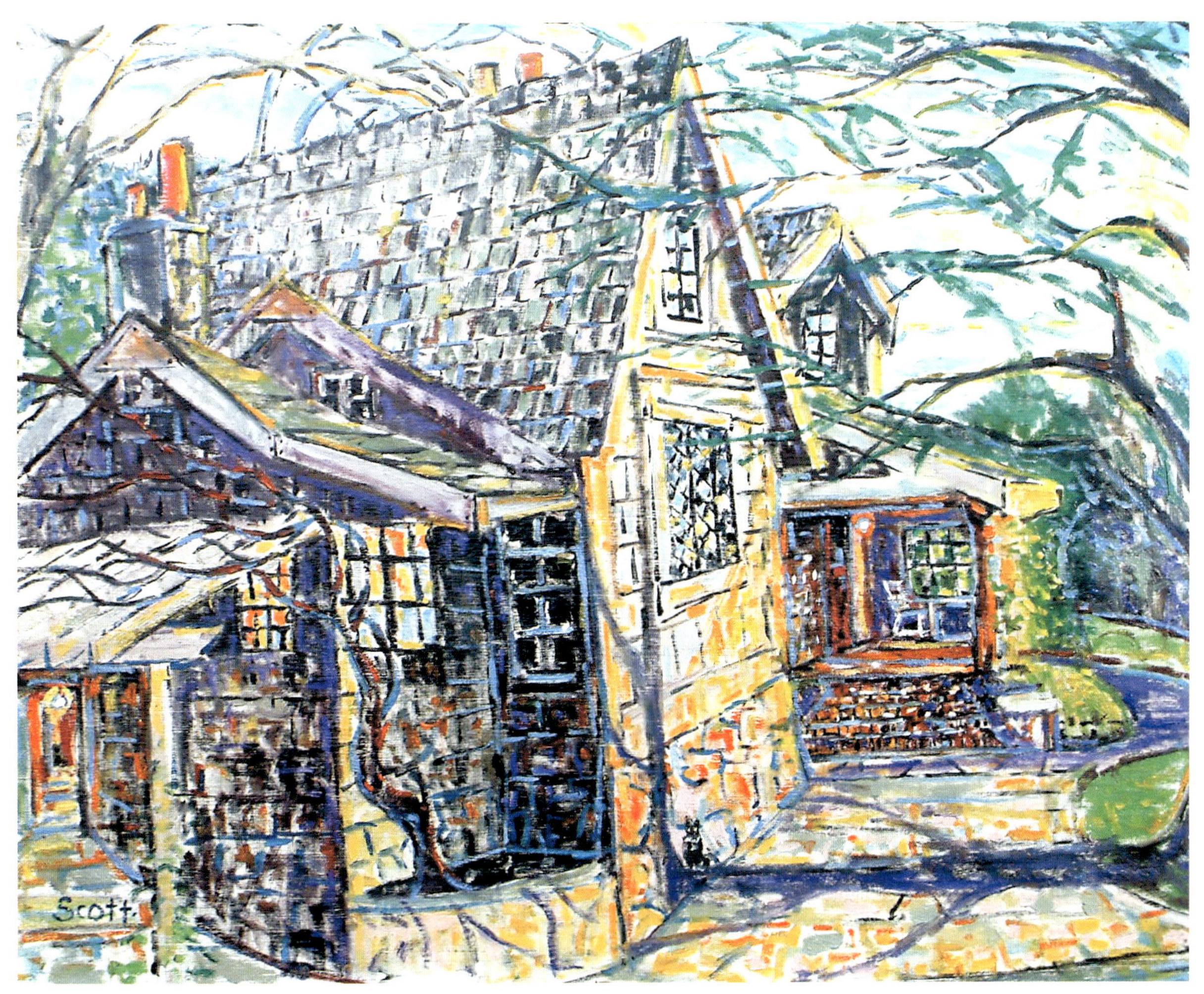

Oil on Panel, 24 x 30 inches. "Filberg Lodge"

The Barrel Room

Estate wineries are springing up like spring daisies all over Vancouver Island, as well as many of the smaller islands in the Gulf. Wineries in the past were restricted to micro-climates in the Victoria area where rain shadow effects from the Olympic Mountains in Washington Sate allowed wine grapes to flourish in tiny agricultural pockets. However, with advances in viniculture, grapes are flourishing in new and ever more varied locations up Island. Hornby and Quadra Island now both boast new wineries.

The 'Barrel Room' is the magical place in a winery operation where the crushed, fermented and aged grape juice is sampled finally as finished wine. Years of hard work and intense nurturing are rewarded when the various vintages are put to the tongue. At this winery, elaborate candle holders have been mounted on the barrels to give the ambient light of romance. Baccus, the Greek God is released from his slumber in the oak barrel room.

In this painting, my imagination has unleashed a full spectrum of colors. Candle light dances across the smooth surface of the oak barrel face. To an artist, the half tone, - the shade between the lightest and darkest colors allow the subconscious mind to emerge and flourish.

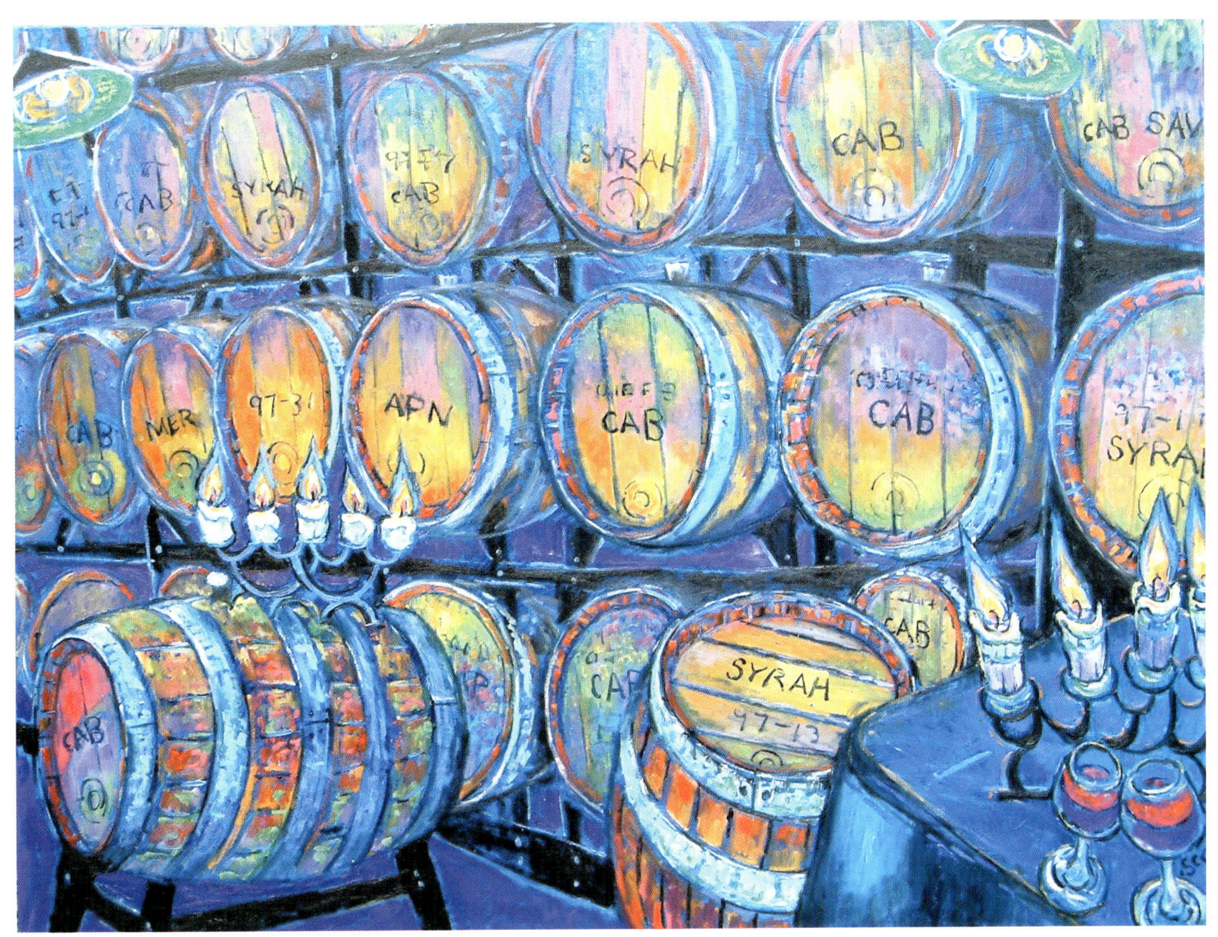

Oil on Canvas, 36 x 48 inches.

Fish Boats Christmas

It was the Romans that first determined their Empire needed a feast or holiday at the Winter Solstice. The Druids followed, with their tradition of illuminating autumn gourds with lights to cut through the bleak darkness. The Christians wisely superimposed Christ's birth on this winter celebration.

Days are short on the West Coast in December,- the wind, wet and damp penetrates the Soul. The First Nations traditionally retreated into their Longhouses during these months, and fell into an orgy of creativity. Everything from totem poles to boxes, rattles to cooking utensils, -even the massive house posts were intricately carved with amazing supernatural creatures during these long winter days inside the Bighouses.

Westcoast harbors at Christmas can also be gloomy and bitterly cold. South-east winds are known to blow for days, and with them come the inevitable driving rain. Fisherman and yachtsmen have started a tradition of lighting up the harbor with the colors of Christmas to fight off the darkness. Many a seaman re-discovers the joy of the season by lighting up their boat's rigging for the holidays, enchanting adults and children alike during these gloomy December weeks.

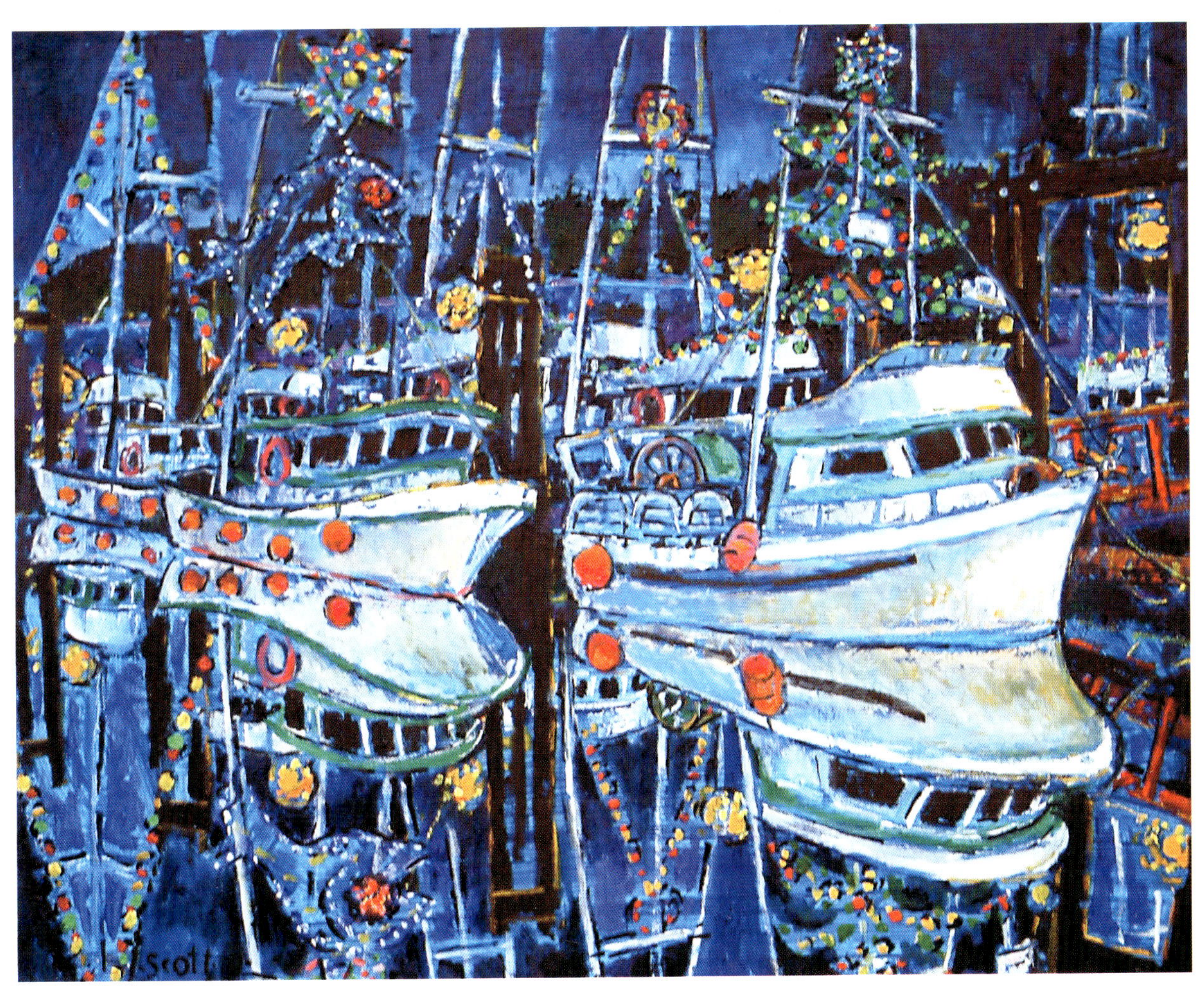

Oil on Panel, 24 x 30 inches.

ChinaTown

The Chinese laborers who came to British Columbia called the province "the Golden Mountain" The Chinese, like many nationalities to this day came to Canada to work hard, long hours, and then go back home and establish themselves with working capital. There are many stories about the opium dens, and illegal gambling, but the full saga is a great deal richer.

Initially, the Chinese were employed to work on the Transcontinental railway. Being versatile, they branched out into gold mining, and the primary service industries. Every town of any size had a 'Chinatown'. Many of the structures were very humble, as the Chinese were the original recyclers. They didn't build permanent structures, since they didn't intend to stay permanently. However in the larger more prosperous communities such as Cumberland in the Comox Valley, they developed hotels, political clubs, -even an Opera House. Vibrant, creative Chinese communities thrived throughout early Vancouver Island.

Being, of course, descended from other thrifty 'Scots' -I admire the Cumberland Chinese community and its approach to hydro bills. They simply devised new wiring for 'Chinatown' - where all their homes were linked electrically to each other, but of course, to only one meter!

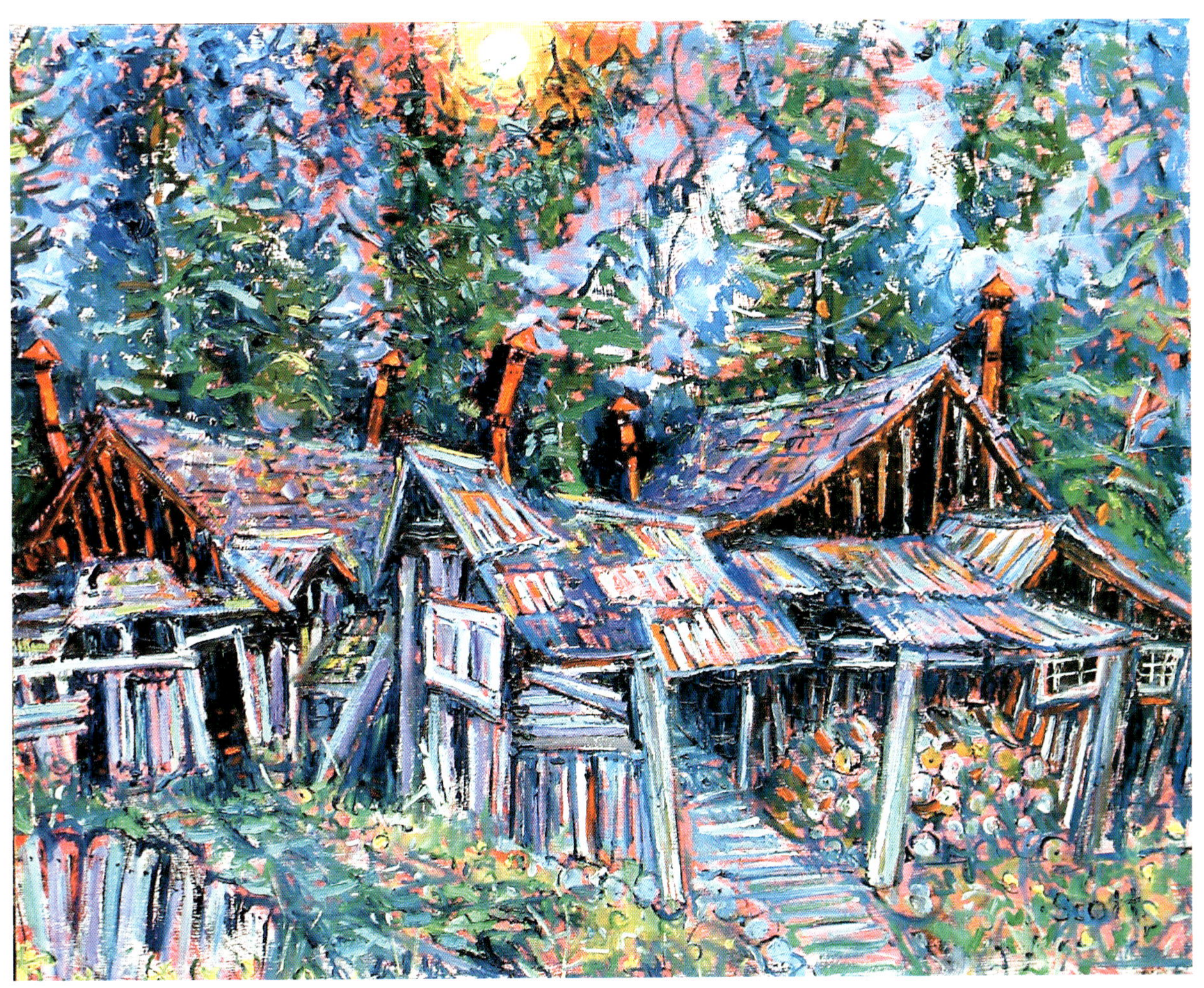

Oil on panel. 24 x 30 inches. "Sunset ChinaTown"

Cape George

The "Cape George" is a classic Westcoast Seine Boat, She fished salmon and herring for over 50 years up and down the Coast. Seine Fishing is very much different from trolling, and similar to gill netting in the sense both kinds of fishing use nets.

The "Purse Seine" literally encircles a school of salmon or herring and completely encloses the catch . Then, with the help of a large barrel, the crew will mechanically haul the fish aboard.

The "Cape George" is being restored in Nanaimo Harbor by the Historical Society. What attracted me to paint this ship was her colors. Douglas fir is the preferred timber for planking on fish boats, for the simple reason it is a very hard wood, the hardest of the softwoods on the coast. Over the years as Doug Fir is repeatedly varnished, it takes on a bright orange color. This, to an artist, is a wonderful contrast to the blues and grays of the ocean.

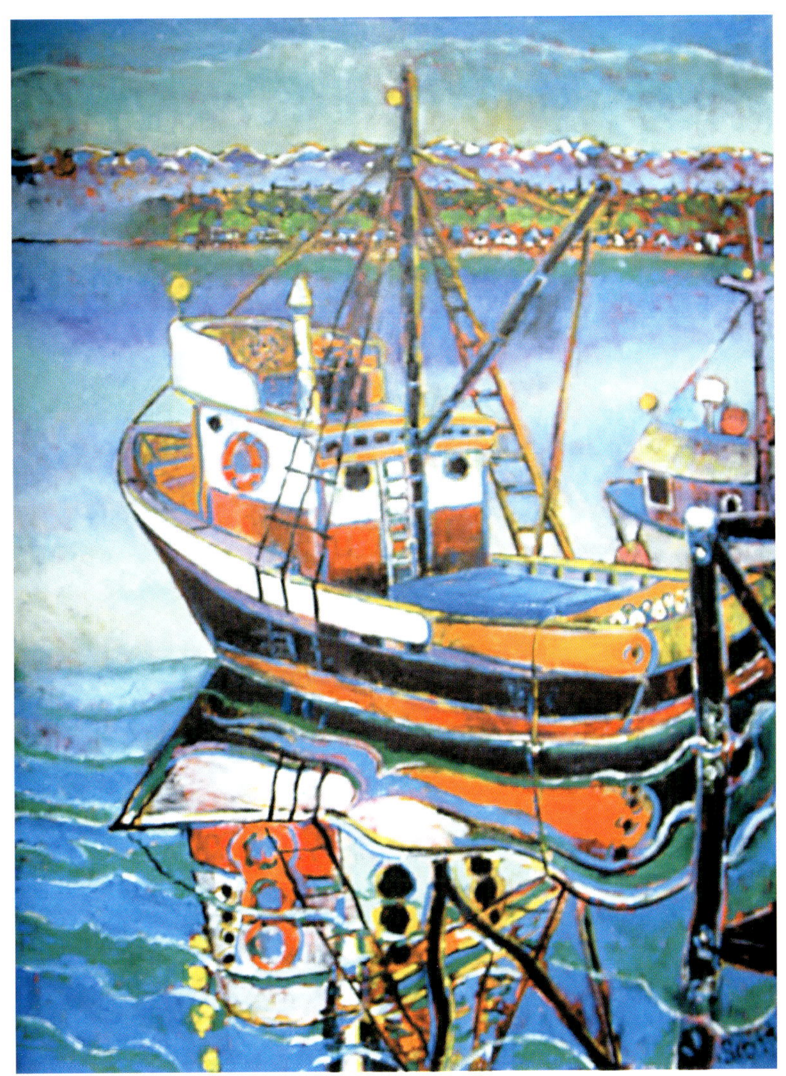

Oil on Canvas, 30 x 40 inches.

Ghost Barns on Vancouver Island

Forest fires are common occurrences on Vancouver Island during the hot, dry Summer period. Particularly destructive fires occurred in 1922 and 1938. The 1922 fire burned from Campbell River to Lewis Park in Courtenay, taking out many of the early farmsteads. That fire was so large as to be visible from many miles away. Cortez Islanders rowed offshore to watch the wall of fire consuming Vancouver Island.

Farms were called 'stump ranches' since the fields were covered with gigantic stumps left after cutting down the old growth forest. Veterans who survived the First World War were given logged off land to farm on Vancouver Island. Ironically, many of these Vets killed themselves trying to blow up the stumps on these little farms. Farming and tragedy were never far apart in pioneer British Columbia.

The "Ghost" barn in this painting, owned by long time resident Nolly Smith survived many great forest fires. It is a relic of the past, and happily lives on, up against the mountains near Burns Bog.

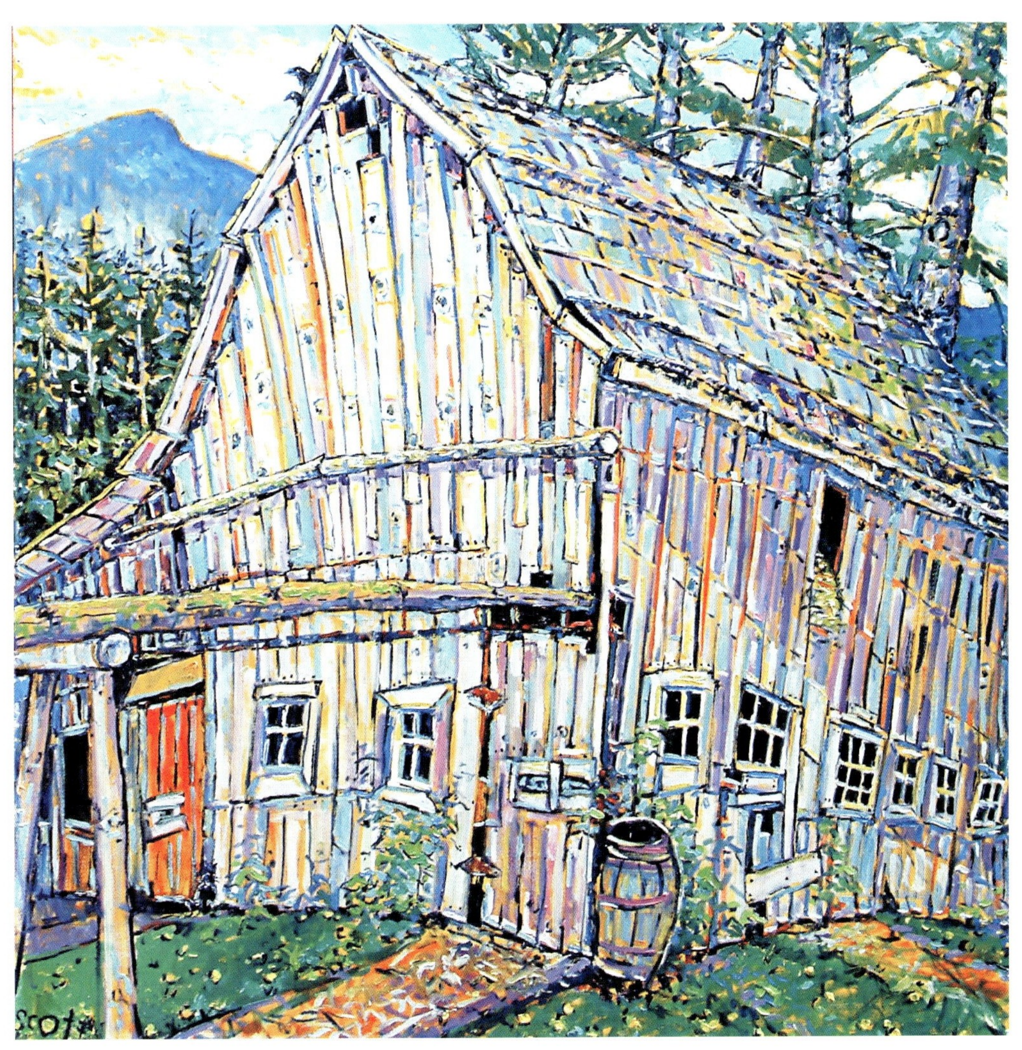

Oil on Canvas, 36 x 36 inches. "Ghost Barn"

The Old House Restaurant, Courtenay

Mike McLaughlin will always be associated with the beginning of the Old House tradition in the Comox Valley. In Courtenay/Comox, if you're celebrating something really special , chances are one of the first places you think of is the Old House.

The restaurant began on the Kirk family homestead along the Courtenay River. The original home was built in 1938. Mike McLaughlin completed the renovations on the home and two acre property to create the restaurant in 1974. The heavily carved post and beam architecture is based on the New England pioneer style with extensive use of leaded windows. Guests can warm away the winter damp by any one of the four stone fireplaces. The cedar shake siding and roof shingles give it a definite West Coast look.

In 1996, the Muir Family made the Old House their own, -and a true family business. Owner Ken Muir is the Pastry Chef, while his wife Marnie lovingly tends the extensive grounds and gardens. Son Kevin has taken on the job as General Manager, and his wife Kaiyo manages the Office details.

And of course, there is Sophie, the dog, who you'll find roaming quietly outside on the grounds. The gardens are particularly spectacular since Marnie and her friend Diane took command. The Old House staff joke that sometimes guests of the garden drop by the restaurant as an afterthought. Each season in the garden is uniquely special, from spring bulbs to fall's rich hues. The Old House gardens have become very popular settings for weddings, anniversaries and birthday photos.

I have painted the Old House many times, and have always enjoyed a day there. It remains a very special place for me.

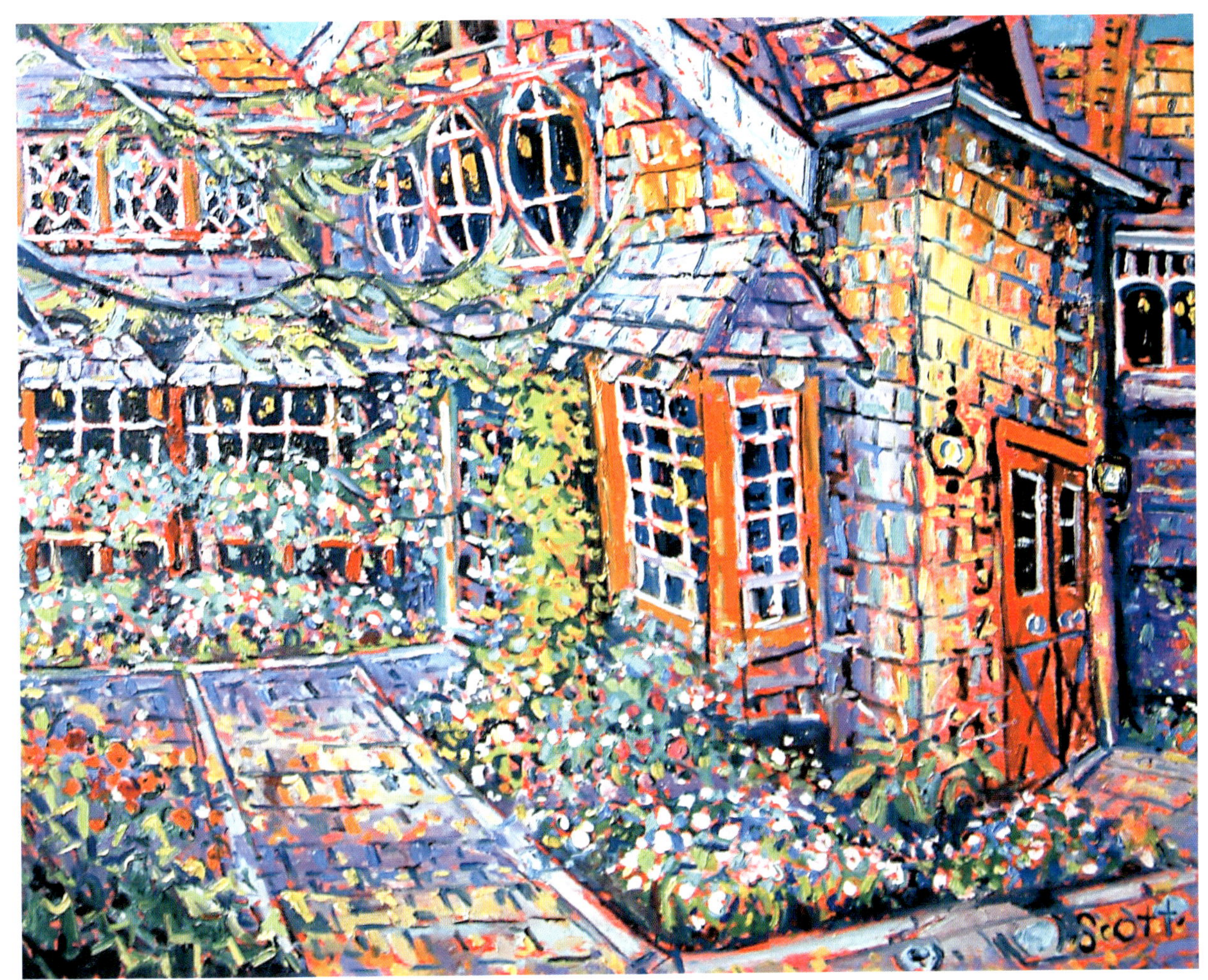

Oil on Panel, 24 x 36 inches. "Old House"

Schooner Restaurant, Tofino

Tofino, on the West Coast of B.C., boasts 1.25 million tourists per year, a testament to the beauty and hospitality of this Vancouver Island location. People from all over the world find their way to this north Pacific playground with its beaches, rugged mountains, hot springs and migrating grey whales.

However, my favorite Schooner story is about a Tanzanian family who met a couple from South Africa while on a cruise ship. The Tanzanians mentioned in conversation that they were about to visit Canada. The South Africans were adamant that their new friends should "Go to British Columbia, visit Vancouver Island, see a town called Tofino on the west coast, go to the Schooner Restaurant and have the steamed Black Cod!." And they did just that. After Mare, the owner and Chef served them this wonderful meal to the guests who had traveled 20,000 km to try it, they assured her that the meal and the scenery were worth the trip! What an amazing testament to Mare's award-winning cuisine.

I love painting the Schooner with its expressionist lines and colors. The sunsets in Tofino are breathtaking, -just what my palette is looking for!

A new exciting expansion in underway in the upstairs of the Schooner that recently housed a craft gallery. A larger and more elegant dining room will give patrons a panoramic view of Tofino Harbor with its fjords, snow-capped mountains and views of Bedwell Glacier. Mare is planning an exciting new menu to tempt your appetites. Doug, her hard-working partner, always has a new story or theory that he will try out on you!

Interestingly, the Schooner Restaurant started out in life as a military hospital during the second world war, and was moved overland to its present site. The old saying "Go West" is never more true than when it comes to a Vancouver Island adventure that ends at the "Schooner" in Tofino.

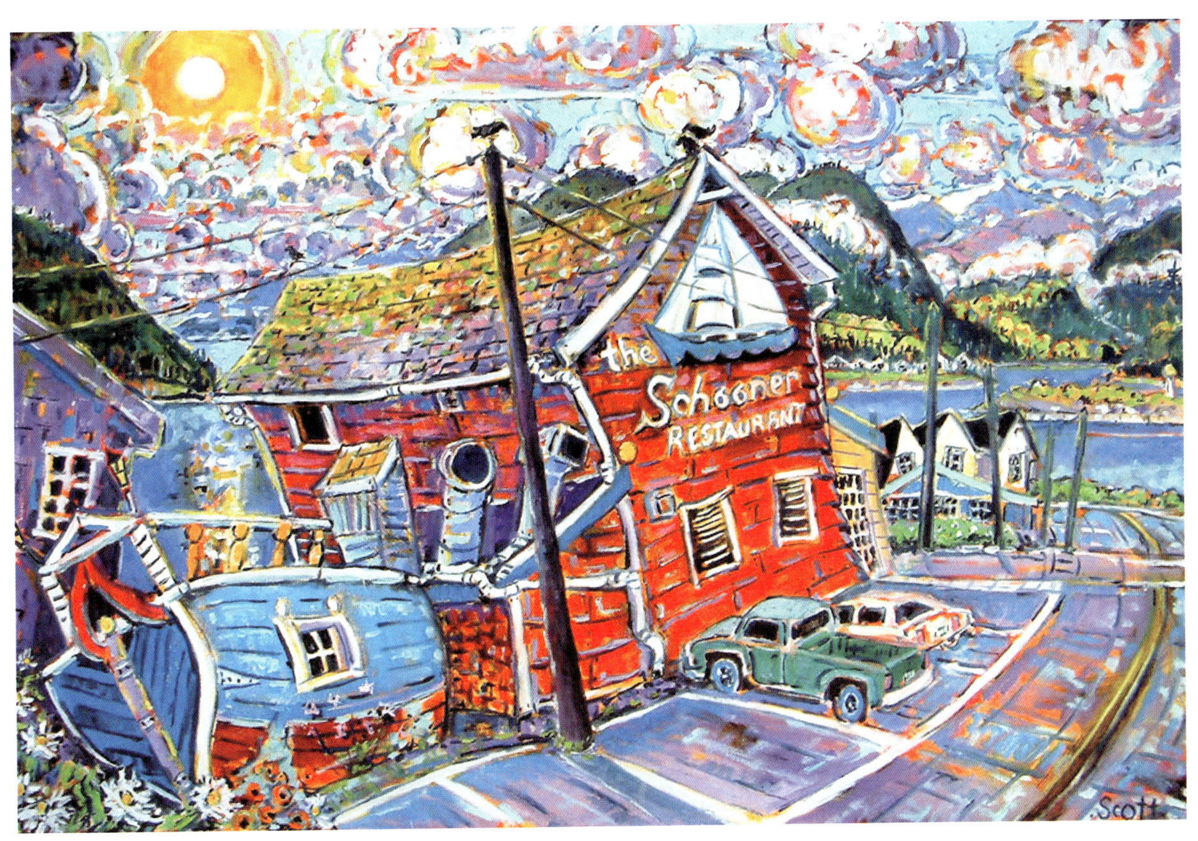

Oil on Canvas 24 x 36 inches

Strathcona Park Lodge

Strathcona Park Lodge is strategically located at the junction of the Upper Campbell and Buttle Lakes , about a thirty minute drive from Campbell River towards Gold River on Vancouver Island. Looking directly at King's Peak, -the Lodge promises, and delivers, spectacular Outdoor Educational facilities and activities. Rock climbing, kayaking, hiking, soothing spa facilities…the possibilities are endless!

Strathcona was created in 1960 as an Outdoor Education Center for kids, which it still provides, -but now 'grown-ups' get to share in the fun. It has become a destination of choice for Vancouver Island visitors. Recently, many brides have been lured by the rugged beauty of the site for their weddings. The rustic cabins on the beach add to the romantic get-away atmosphere, allowing everyone to completely relax.

The Lodge, and its outbuildings, are a throw back to an earlier time when life was simpler. Guests can eat communally and there is a strong sense of community and cooperation. The craggy buildings were all hand built with a lot of TLC, with great fun put into the details. The original property was a 'stump ranch' -a barren piece of land with nothing but enormous tree stumps left in the ground from previous logging operations, and huge piles of slash, -massive labyrinths of branches. Time has been kind to the property, and now it is a spectacular, rejuvenated forest setting with breath-taking mountain vistas. The sunsets there are truly some of the best in B.C.!

Originally Jim and Myrna Boulding started the Lodge, but it has become a wonderfully diverse family operation, with many kids and grandkids involved! Over the years, the growing issues of wilderness Recreation have been addressed by Brian Gunn, who, with Myrna, continue to be the 'guardians of the gate' at Strathcona Park Lodge.

A visit to their spectacular facility is sure to reward a visitor with a friendly greeting, in a magnificent setting.

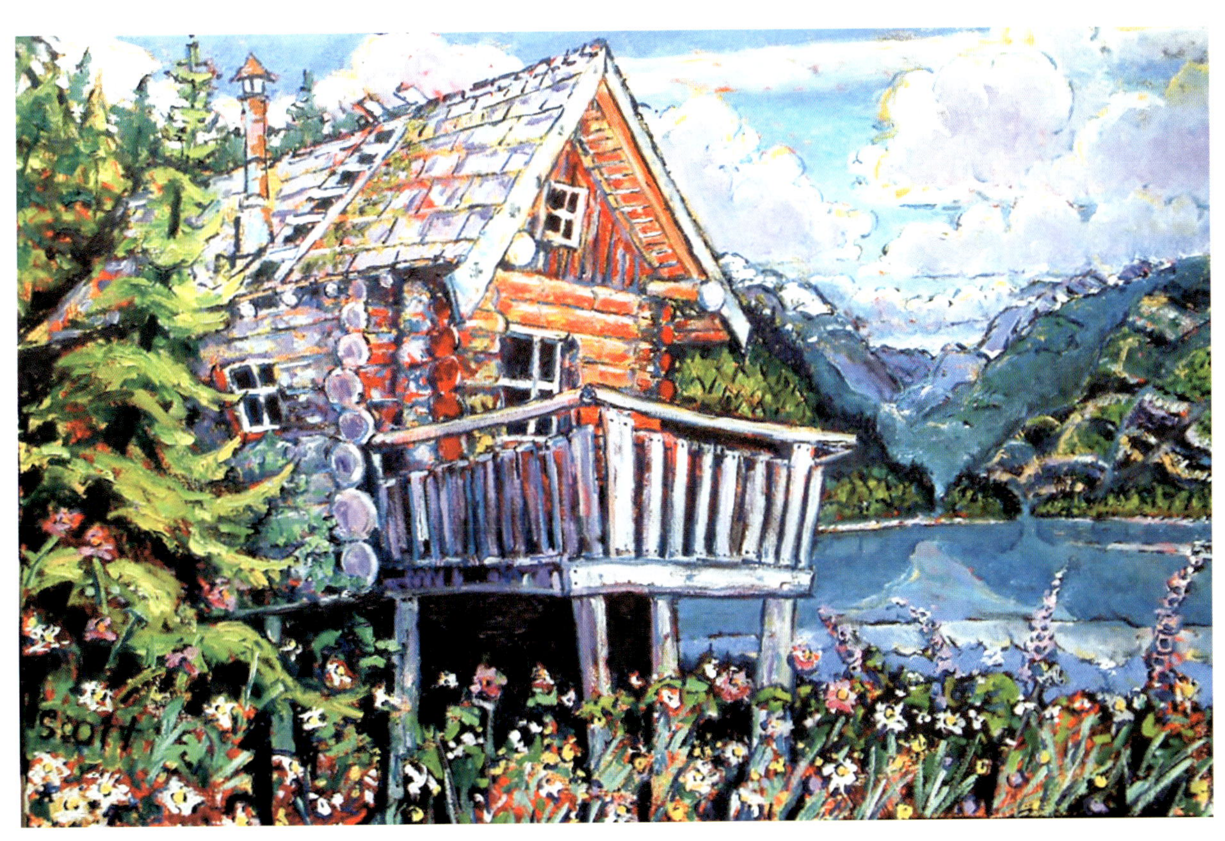

Oil on Canvas   24x36 inches